# FROM PATHETIC TO PROPHETIC

BY

CAROLYN PRISCILLA BYNUM

"We also have the prophetic message as something completely reliable, and you will do well to pay attention to it, as to a light shining in a dark place, until the day dawns and the morning star rises in your hearts."

2 Peter 1:19, NIV

LIFE TO LEGACY

From Pathetic to Prophetic

By: Carolyn P. Bynum, Copyright © 2017

ISBN-13 978-1-947288-24-9

ISBN-10 1-947288-24-5

Printed in the United States

10 9 8 7 6 5 4 3 2 1

Cover design by:  Legacy Design Inc
                 Legacydesigninc@gmail.com

Published by: Life To Legacy, LLC
15255 S. 94th Ave, 5th Floor
Orland Park, IL 60462
877-267-7477
Life2legacybooks@att.net

# CONTENTS

# CONTENTS (Continued)

# ACKNOWLEDGMENTS

To My Beloved, Jesus Christ the Lord and the Spirit of Truth Who reveals Him to me as it pleases my Heavenly Father.

To Bishop Paul E. Bynum, Sr., my husband of 40 years, our sons Xavier and Paul and our four grandchildren. Mileena Kathryn, Jade Alexandria, Alyssa Monet, and Elizabeth Caroline: Through each of you, I experience so much of God's love and blessings. I am among the happiest wives, mothers, and grandmothers on the planet.

To Mary Anna, Frances, Wilma, and Richard: I am greatly enriched, loved, and blessed indeed to be your sister.

In loving memory of my father Richard, my mother, Lillian, sister, Grace and infant brothers, George William and James Michael.

To the Family at Restoration Christian Ministries, Sierra Vista, Arizona and the Body of Christ throughout the Kingdom: Walk in the Spirit and you will receive Power to become the sons of God.

Grace, peace, love, thanks and blessings to all.

# FOREWORD

*But when it pleased God, who separated me from my mother's womb, and called me by his grace,*
*To reveal his <u>Son in me</u>, that I might preach him among the heathen; immediately*
*<u>I conferred not with flesh and blood</u>.*
Galatians 1:15-16

Carolyn P. Bynum is a servant of God the Father, our Lord Jesus Christ and also my wife. She is a pastor, teacher, and songwriter of the Lord, and the best gift God could give to a man. I am proud and honored to be her husband of 41 years. We have two sons and four granddaughters.

Pastor Carolyn, as we all refer to her in Restoration Christian Ministries Center, has always served the Lord with her beautiful and anointed voice, but now with the sharing of the Gospel (Good News) for 23 years. With the Lord's anointed teaching, she has set many captives free, healed the sick, and brought knowledge to many by the Spirit of the Word, starting with me.

Pastor Carolyn has the respect of many sons of God with me being the first. She has my support in all that she does and wants to do forever. It is my pleasure and honor to serve the Lord with her in ministry. Forever together in spirit and love, Bishop Paul E. Bynum, Sr.

# INTRODUCTION

This author endeavors to be ever Christ-centered. This undertaking became far less challenging once I learned total dependence upon the Holy Spirit to reveal Him. Shall we begin with the fact that the Lord of Hosts raised up a Prophet for His people, and we are to listen to Him. That Prophet is Jesus Christ the Righteous. God put His Words in the mouth of His Prophet, and His Prophet has spoken all that God commanded. As the Word, He did not return to the Father void, but accomplished all He was sent to do. We may be certain for it is written that the Father announced, "This is my beloved Son, in whom I am well pleased; hear ye Him (Matthew 17:5)." Further, the Book of Hebrews leaves no doubt that God, in these last days has spoken to us by His Son (1:2).

Today, many are listening to the shallow words of the wisdom of men instead of the Life-sustaining Word of the true Prophet. Enabled to see the magnitude of this shortfall, it is most alarming to true prophetic ministry. While there should not be a feeble one among us, the state of the Church in many places is lamentable. What is being called ministry for some is miserably inadequate. As Jesus proclaimed on the last day of the Feast of Tabernacles in John Chapter 7, He is the Source from which a thirsty one can drink and be filled. He is the One if believed on Who will cause living water or the Spirit to flow from our bellies. While there were some present who doubted, this proclamation caused many to acknowledge that He was indeed the Prophet. In another instance on the road to Emmaus, Jesus was called a prophet mighty in deed and word in the sight of God and all the people (Luke 24:19). Indeed, He is!

It is most distressing the volume of "prophetic ministry" ongoing that blatantly excludes The Prophet. As children of God, we cannot become foolish having begun in the Spirit then attempt to go into the fullness of Christ on our own! The term "prophetic" in many places has become synonymous with fortune telling.

Our "fortune" is the blessed privilege of Life in Christ! One must get an understanding of the Scripture which declares, we have this *treasure* in earthen vessels, so that the surpassing greatness of the power will be of God and not from ourselves (2 Corinthians 4:7). We are holy coffers, but many know it not because they walk after the flesh and not after the Spirit. Have we not read and believe that God shall supply all our need according to His riches in glory by Christ Jesus? These riches exceed any and all earthly "fortune."

The testimony of Jesus is the spirit of prophecy (Revelation 19:10), and we are complete in Him which is the Head of all principality and power (Colossians 2:10). Where then is the necessity for the excess static and clamor from man's psyche? What has brought about the gross desensitization to the rhetoric of the false prophet? What can man possibly devise that is able to eclipse the glory of the Son of God? Why are world events presented in competition with the Power of the Cross of Christ? Why is the spirit of fear overwhelming many that have been given a spirit of love, power, and a sound mind (2 Timothy 1:7)? Why are many star-gazing instead of embracing the Star of Jacob (Numbers 24:17)? That Star is The Messiah; the Highest; the Daystar risen in our hearts; and the Bright and Morning Star! He is the only One able to bring Mazzaroth (the twelve signs of the Zodiac) in his season, guide the constellations, and knows the ordinances of heaven (Job 38:32-33). Did we forget to be of good cheer because Christ Jesus overcame the world (John 16:33)? His is the Kingdom, the Power and the Glory!

There are many powerful examples of prophets in the Bible. Believers who receive the blessing of Jesus that greater works we will do because He went to the Father know there is something most powerful that is sorely missing in the Church today. For many, a restlessness is in the atmosphere, and the rumbling of spiritual hunger pangs is being heard. Sons are wide awake and seeking to enter nothing less than the fullness of Christ. Our spirits must be in the one and only place where they can thrive. That place is Christ.

Jesus is the best Example of a prophet one will ever find, especially when addressing a need in His Church. Any need outside of Him is death and Resurrection Life is the only remedy. To help unveil the Divine Ability that is true of us in Him even now, let us lay Jesus, the Holy Pattern, over the prophetic ministry of the prophet Elisha. Elisha's life and ministry anointed with a double portion will become a clarion trumpet to convey the urgency of the message of this hour when seen through the eyes of the Spirit. Greater works are about to manifest!

*I will raise up for them a prophet like you from among their fellow Israelites, and I will put my words in his mouth. He will tell them everything I command him.*
*Deuteronomy 18:18, NIV*

# CHAPTER 1

## THE CALL AND ANOINTING OF ELISHA

Elijah was instructed by God to anoint Elisha in his stead (1 Kings 19:16). *Stead* as used here is one of those words in Scripture for which there is no easy definition. In fact, Strong's Concordance did not attempt to define it. From Elisha's ministry one can determine that not only was the spirit of Elijah upon him, but he also had a double portion of his spirit. Line that fact up with Jesus' declaration of John 14:12, "He that believeth on me, the works that I do shall he do also; and greater *works* than these shall he do; because I go unto my Father." Therefore, one can be sure the term *in his stead* means more than an alternate or substitute.

It is most intriguing that at the same time Elisha was anointed prophet, Jehu, whose name means *Jehovah is He*, was anointed king over Israel. His father, Nimshi means *rescued*. Elisha, meaning *God is salvation*, was the son of Shaphat or *judged*. Unlike Jehu, Elisha's father's homeland is named. The God-inspired language of the Scriptures includes His empowering strategies. Elisha's father was from Abelmeholah. It means *meadow of dancing*. One meaning of dance is to whirl or prepare *to mount up*. Oh my!

Abelmeholah is also a city of Issachar whose sons were men that had understanding of the times to know what Israel ought to do (1 Chronicles 12:32). How critical such an anointed ministry is needed today! By now a most grand picture of an exalted spiritual position in Christ should be coming into focus. We are being established in a present truth. In sum, God is ruling over His people who have been rescued by His Son, Jesus. We are saved and have been judged in righteousness in Christ. We rejoice in Him and as we mount up in the Spirit, we operate from a realm of greater works through a double portion Anointing.

Elijah found Elisha plowing with twelve yoke of oxen before him, and he with the twelfth. Envision one in a season of preparation for his call and all that is before him is that which speaks to the government of God. Take a moment to absorb what is before us in very simple terms. With what speaks to the government of God (twelve), Elisha is plowing or turning earth. He is breaking up fallow ground. According to the prophet Hosea, this speaks of sowing to ourselves in righteousness so we may reap in mercy. It should also remind one that now is the time to seek the LORD until He comes and rains righteousness upon us (Hosea 10:12). Elijah passed by Elisha, and cast his mantle upon him.

We all must allow the authority of God to completely turn the earth of our hearts. As this happens by faith, our double portion is on its way to us. Reconsider that while Elisha was engaged in this activity, Elijah cast his mantle upon him. Mark well that there is a lot that will transpire between the time the mantle is cast upon us and the beginning of the ministry of the double portion in our lives. It is a season of preparation for leadership. Let us not make the mistake of many and try to rush this Divine Process in Christ.

Elisha served Elijah until Elijah's ascension. The reader is encouraged to study 2 Kings Chapters 2 through 6 very carefully to enhance understanding of how God revealed Himself in the ministry of Elisha. As a minister unto Elijah, Elisha followed him without wavering. So must we follow Christ! Let us monitor the events regarding Elijah's ascension.

When the time came for Elijah to be taken up into heaven by a whirlwind, Elijah went with Elisha to Gilgal. Gilgal received its name when God told Joshua, "This day have I rolled away the reproach of Egypt from off you (Joshua 5:9)." Oh what power this all starts out with! Elijah accompanied Elisha to Gilgal indicating for us the reproach of the world system and all its bondage has been rolled away in Redemption.

Elijah told Elisha to remain at Gilgal because God had sent him to Bethel. Elisha emphatically stated that he was not leaving Elijah. See, once the mantle of Anointing touches, the truly called out one knows there is no stopping short of entering all Christ's fullness. Many have camped at what Gilgal speaks to, but there is much more to enter into in Christ. Like Elisha, the pure in heart know that as long as God and their soul lives, they must continue. So Elijah and Elisha went to Bethel which means the *house of God*.

At Bethel, sons of the prophets asked Elisha if he knew the Lord was going "to take his master from his head that day." Elisha responded in the affirmative and told them to hold their peace. Along our developmental journey, there will be those who can rehearse a situation but have not a clue what it means spiritually. With titles in tow, they know nothing of spiritual things. Tell them to hold their peace and follow on to know the Lord.

Elijah was moving on to Jericho and Elisha would not leave him though again bidden to tarry at Bethel. Jericho is a place that means *moon*. It can speak to that which has no light of its own but brightly reflects the light of the sun. Again, Elisha was confronted by sons of the prophets there and asked the identical question, "Knowest thou that the LORD will take away thy master from thy head today?" The side chatter of others must not be allowed to distract. Again, Elisha told them to hold their peace.

As the Body of Christ, we are confident that He is the Head. He has the preeminence in all things, and all fullness dwells in Him (Colossians 1:18-19). Are you in a place where sons of the prophets only have questions but no answers? Hopefully, not. Elisha knows Elijah will be taken, but he will not let go of the blessing of his master that will be later magnified upon and within himself.

Elijah headed for Jordan. Again, Elisha did not tarry, but the two of them went on together. Elisha was yet proclaiming he would not leave Elijah as long as God and his soul lived. As Elijah and Elisha stood by Jordan, fifty men of the sons of the prophets went to watch from afar off. The positioning of the sons of the prophets is an indication of their spiritual immaturity. Many are putting distance between the might of the Spirit and themselves. They watch from afar. It is equivalent to knowing Jesus was crucified while having no understanding that we were crucified together with Him (Galatians 2:20). May all come into the knowledge of the Apostle Paul's revelation of that very truth.

Another point that must be addressed at this point and throughout concerns the immaturity of the sons of the prophets. Their lack of understanding will be very obvious during the ministry of Elisha. For now, hear what the Lord is saying through them to us presently. We have established that they first appear at Bethel meaning the house of God. They were not mentioned at Gilgal, the place of rolling our reproach away. Gilgal is what we all experience before we come into the house of God. Once in the house of God, they appear and begin to speak of spiritual things but without revelation. All they can do is to ask Elisha the same question, "Knowest thou that the LORD will take away thy master from thy head today?" They know an event is going to take place, but they do not know what it means. We will address this again later also.

They are also present at Jericho, and the same thing happened as at Bethel. Remember, Jericho means moon, which only reflects light. The sons of the prophets at Jericho represent those not yet filled with the Light. Now at Jordan, a specific number of them is mentioned. Fifty. Fifty is the number of Pentecost or that which speaks to the Spirit. The sons of the prophets are not operating in the power of the Spirit, but they certainly are about to see a manifestation like never before.

Elijah took his mantle, wrapped it together and smote the waters. The waters divided, and he and Elisha went over Jordan on dry ground. Cross Jordan and some requests may be made known! Jordan speaks to the death of self, and crossing it on dry ground means Resurrection Life is in operation. At this place, the anointed minister knows to ask according to the will of God. There are no carnal requests here. Things are all-powerful, and it is all onward and upward. Here is what a right request looks like. Elijah asked Elisha what he should do for him before he was taken, and Elisha asked Elijah to let a double portion of his spirit be upon him. The asking was a *hard thing* according to Elijah, but the requirement to receiving the answer was simple and totally spiritual. Elisha had to *see* Elijah when he was taken from him.

Faith keeps moving so as Elijah and Elisha went on and talked, heaven was opened, and there appeared a chariot of fire and horses of fire and parted them. Sometimes faith literally shoves us into a blessing. Elijah went up by a whirlwind into heaven, and lo and behold Elisha saw it! Elisha's response sheds great light on what he saw by the Spirit. He said, "My father, my father, the chariot of Israel, and the horsemen thereof."

The chariot of Israel and the horsemen are not natural but spiritual! Those looking for a white horse to appear in the sky need to soberly hear what the Spirit is saying now. That day, Elisha knew he was a son of God, and so are we in Christ for it is written in Galatians 4:6, "*And because ye are sons, God hath sent forth the Spirit of his Son into your hearts, crying, Abba (Father), Father.*" We have received the Spirit of adoption, whereby we cry, Abba (Father), Father (Romans 8:15). Just as Jesus, our Elder Brother said in His obedience unto death for our sakes, "*Abba, Father, all things are possible unto thee; take away this cup from me: nevertheless not what I will, but what thou wilt* (Mark 14:36)." Behold, a son!

*In the last days, God says, I will pour out my Spirit on all people. Your sons and daughters will prophesy, your young men will see visions, your old men will dream dreams. Even on my servants, both men and women, I will pour out my Spirit in those days, and they will prophesy.*

*Acts 2: 17-18, NIV*

# CHAPTER 2

## KNOW HIM NO MORE AFTER THE FLESH

Elisha did not see Elijah anymore. Although he did not see Elijah, he received a double portion of his spirit. Faith is the catalyst from here on. Many continually attempt to see Jesus naturally. He is not to be seen or known after the flesh anymore (2 Corinthians 5:16). When Jesus was about to be glorified, some Greeks requested to see Him. He gave an Eternal reply to their request. "Very truly I tell you, unless a kernel of wheat falls to the ground and dies, it remains only a single seed. But if it dies, it produces many seeds. Anyone who loves their life will lose it, while anyone who hates their life in this world will keep it for eternal life. Whoever serves me must follow me; and where I am, my servant also will be. My Father will honor the one who serves me (John 12:24-26)."

Compare Jesus' response to what one may hear from many today. Instead of scheduling an audience to impart some carnal, temporal, ineffective action or seeking the glory and fame the pride of life flaunts, one must put on the Mind of Christ. From now on He is to be seen in His Body as One with Him and Father. As Elisha is preparing to minister in the Power and Authority of Almighty God, we must move out in the same Power. Nothing less will bring glory to God. All things are new here!

Elisha took off his own clothes and rent them in two pieces and took up the mantle of Elijah that fell from him and went back and stood by Jordan. By taking off his own clothes, he relinquished himself to the full authority of that taken up. With Elijah's mantle, Elisha smote the waters and said, "Where is the Lord God of Elijah?" The water parted and Elisha went over. Greater works have commenced.

Faith is in full operation. At first, Elisha had faith to minister unto Elijah. From the moment Elijah encountered him plowing and cast his mantle on him, he was drawn to follow him. There was a Divine Exchange. A hunger for something from above began to drive Elisha from that moment on. That hunger became so intense, Elisha desired and received a double portion of Elijah's spirit. Do not stop! Never give up!

Many today have no revelation of what seeing Elijah taken means. If people had understanding of it, they would embrace the Cross of Christ. Seeing the chariot of Israel and the horsemen thereof means he actually experienced heaven invading earth. Just as the whirlwind took Elijah, the same Rushing Wind or Spirit of God came in fullness at Pentecost. Receive the Holy Spirit! Jesus' Mantle has fallen but few take It up! When we receive the Holy Spirit, Resurrection Life begins within. The first thing people should notice, just as with Elisha, that we have conquered death or smote the waters of Jordan and they divided.

Jesus ascended on high and gave gifts to men. Stated another way, Jesus dispersed Himself in the form of apostles, prophets, evangelists, pastors and teachers. Instead of taking Him up, people have grabbed titles and corralled people unto themselves without a notion of what is true of them spiritually. According to Ephesians 4, these gifts are given till His people grow up into the measure of the stature of His fullness. If that is not happening in one's ministry, then that person should step aside and give Christ His rightful place. His Spirit alone should be functioning in one whether an apostle, prophet, evangelist, pastor or teacher.

All of us in ministry should be spiritually answering the question of "Where is the God and Father of our Lord Jesus Christ? Notice the emphasis on answering not asking! We should be blessing Him Who has blessed us with all spiritual blessings in heavenly places in Christ (Ephesians 1). According to His abundant mercy, He has begotten us again unto a living hope by His Resurrection from the dead to an inheritance incorruptible. This inheritance is undefiled, does not fade away, and is reserved in heaven for us (1 Peter 1:3-4). Christ in Power of His Resurrection should be on full display no matter what the ministry is. How can we minister in power if we have not come back in Resurrection Power from being crucified with Christ? That is what crossing Jordan epitomizes.

Any anointed minister of righteousness will evidently have the Power of Christ upon them. In the Scriptures one will notice the sons of the prophets at Jericho said the spirit of Elijah is resting on Elisha (2 Kings 2:15). It was evident! They came to meet Elisha and bowed before him. They knew the spirit of Elijah was upon Elisha, but they did not see Elijah taken. This is a serious problem in ministry today because these same people are ministering to God's people. The first thing they desire to do is to help with something they do not understand. They were fifty strong probably indicating another spirit but not the Holy Spirit. They wanted to look for Elisha's master, Elijah, who in their view may have been taken up by the Spirit of the Lord and cast upon some mountain or in some valley. Hear the pathetic mixture as though the Spirit of God is incapable of facilitating ascension.

See the travesty? People know something spiritual has taken place, but they have not the clarity of it. Spirit-filled ministers are endued to bring clarity! The actions of these sons of the prophets at Jericho are almost laughable until one is sobered by the fact that people today, in the same manner, do not know what happened to their Master, Jesus Christ our Lord, either. They obviously lack understanding because they are seeking Him after the flesh or in the natural in all the wrong places instead of by the Spirit.

Elisha warned them not to send to look for Elijah. They continued to press Elisha until he permitted them. Sometimes people do not respond to spiritual instruction and waste a lot of time doing things according to their own understanding. We do not control people but rather patiently instruct. To attempt to control them is actually witchcraft. So, they sent fifty men, again speaking to a powerless spirit in operation, and looked for three days and of course, did not find Elijah.

A three-day journey taken in the Spirit will produce the answer. See again the ineffective ministry of moving without the Holy Spirit. They reported back to Elisha as if they had some news, and Elisha admonished them because he told them not to send to look for Elijah in the first place. Notice from Scripture that Elisha did not let them go on a wild goose chase and leave them hanging. He waited at Jericho until they saw for themselves and returned. Such instances happen to true ministry to teach patience or longsuffering. Remember, we are all in Divine Process. Love must wait.

*We also have the prophetic message as something completely reliable, and you will do well to pay attention to it, as to a light shining in a dark place, until the day dawns and the morning star rises in your hearts.*
*2 Peter 1: 19 (NIV)*

# CHAPTER 3

### HEALING OF THE WATER

After parting Jordan, Elisha's next ministry experience dealt with the water and the ground. The people lived in a place that was beautifully situated, but the water was bad, and the ground was barren. Such is the condition in many places in the Church today. There are buildings of beautiful architecture furnished most elaborately incorporating the latest in technology, but the water is bad, and the land is unfruitful. The water speaks to the Word being ministered which should have its Source as the Spirit, but since it does not, it is bad or evil. The people are drinking from carnal reasoning, and they are unable to bear spiritual fruit. Look around and survey the lack of love, joy, peace, longsuffering, gentleness, goodness, faith, meekness and temperance (Galatians 5:22-23). If there is no water or Word ministered by the Spirit, there will definitely be no fruit.

Christ is the answer and Elisha knows that in Spirit all things are become new. He asked to be brought a <u>new</u> cruse, which is a jar or bowl. They were to put salt in it. View *salt* in light of Colossians 4:6 which reads, "Let your speech *be* always with grace, seasoned with salt, that ye may know how ye ought to answer every man." A picture is then that of grace which makes the life savory to God and man. Salt is also a preservative and opposes substances that corrupt. If only the Gospel or Word being preached was seasoned with God's grace, the land or His Church would be most bountiful. (We will look closer at the significance of salt in subsequent chapters when we address the resurrection miracles of Jesus).

Elisha went to the spring of the waters to cast the salt in. The spring is the place of going forth or the beginning or source. What an important point! One cannot start in the middle of a religious mess, but rather at the Holy Beginning with all things new in Christ and allow His grace to be ministered to His people. Once grace or salt is cast into the Source of the waters or Word from a new vessel, God's will is set in motion, and He declares the waters healed and all death and barrenness cease. Notice when reading 2 Kings 2, the waters were healed *to this day* according to the saying of Elisha. Elisha words were God's Words just like Jesus! Hear it well!

Consider the fact that the people were unable of themselves to heal the waters, but they had the means within. May every ear hear it! They provided the new cruse and the salt. Christ Jesus has provided all that is necessary for life and healing in Himself. However, what He has given us must be given back to Him and ministered in righteousness. Each of us is a new cruse because Jesus has made all things new. "Therefore if any man *be* in Christ, *he is* a new creature: old things are passed away; behold, all things are become new (2 Corinthians 5:17)." Grace and truth came by Jesus Christ. Salt or grace was there but was not being appropriated. A Spirit-filled minister knows exactly what is required when the water or Word is bad. They preach Christ and Him crucified and what that means to us by the Holy Spirit. They preach the sufficiency of His grace and the perfection of strength in weakness. Is that not precisely what we just saw in Elisha's second miracle?

*Tongues, then, are a sign, not for believers but for unbelievers; prophecy, however, is not for unbelievers but for believers.*
*1 Corinthians 14:22, NIV*

# CHAPTER 4

⚜

## *TWO SHE BEARS*

Elisha left Jericho and went up to Bethel or the house of God. While on the way, little children came out of the city and mocked him saying, "Go up thou bald head, go up thou bald head (2 Kings 2:23)." Elisha turned back and looked on them and cursed them in the name of the Lord. Two she bears came out of the woods and tore 42 of the children. The religious mind is wondering what to make of this situation. Why did the man of God respond in such a manner from the ridicule of children? The spiritual situation here is magnanimous but enshrouded. Let us be guided by the Spirit.

Little children here are actually young men. Young men are not fully mature, spiritually. The term they used saying *"Go up"* means the same as ascend and may have referred to Elijah's translation. If so, this would have been tantamount to blasphemy. They were not only insulting Elisha but God as well. Could it have been that Elijah's spirit was so strong upon Elisha in the face of these immature ones they saw Elijah instead and wanted to see Spirit's power with carnal eyes? What a spiritually sensible alternate view! Historians   have noted that chronologically speaking, Elisha lived 50 more years after this event. The Hebrew word used for little children here is the same word used for Isaac at age 28, Joseph at age 39 and Rehoboam at age 40. Now, are we beginning to see what is happening spiritually?

Put in today's setting in some places, people often ask God to show them His glory while content in their carnal settings. They cry out and carry on incessantly without success because our God is Spirit and will be worshipped in spirit and in truth. How many have gone to crusades not to worship God but to see a sign or miracle? As Jesus said, a wicked and adulterous generation seeks such. Today, young men are still mocking and toying with an all-powerful Event that can only be discerned by the Spirit of the Living God. As long as one is selling "prophecies," he or she is too saying indirectly, *Go up, bald head*! Did you ever read or hear that Jesus Christ of Nazareth did such a thing? You are mocking an Eternal Power, and God is not pleased. In Christ's Love, please stop it.

As a critical interruption at this point, Christ Jesus is being unveiled from within His Body and immature ones will not know what to do but mock. Mocking is equivalent in seriousness to persecution as see between Ishmael and Isaac. Comparing Genesis 21:9 and Gal 4:29 one sees the account of Sarah noticing Ishmael, son of an Egyptian woman, mocking Isaac, the son of the promise. When that same account is recapitulated in the New Testament, the word *mocking* is replaced with *persecution*.

Just as Elisha's experience with the children, there will be no doubting that what is seen upon the vessel is actually the Spirit, so some will attempt to have the vessel do something to please their itching ears and sensual minds. We are not magicians doing tricks for entertainment. We must follow the Spirit at all times and do only what we hear Him say. We must fear God and not man. We are not show-offs from the Kingdom but rather a kingdom of priests who minister in the Power of the Holy Spirit. We seek for God to be glorified in us rather than to us all the time.

Elisha turned back and looked on these young men and cursed them in the Name of the Lord. What place does such blasphemy have in the things of God? Only that which fits in Spirit will be in Spirit! As we proceed, we will see it is the sin that God hates and definitely not His people. What we are seeing is the righteousness of the judgment of God. Notice what happened next. Two she bears came out of the woods and tore forty and two children of them.

Woods speak to humanity. The word bear has a root meaning *to cause to speak*. Notice there are two bears indicating witness. We have so pitifully underestimated the Power of the spoken Word of God. To preach Truth with the fierceness of a she bear cannot help but rend or tear flesh or carnality to pieces. To tear is also to divide as we should be rightly dividing the Word of Truth (2 Timothy 2:15). A bear is slow but methodical. Can we not see that flesh or self has no place in spiritual matters, and God wants us to live in Power being strong in spirit, filled with wisdom, and having His grace upon us? Flesh fully denies this blessed Power and must go!

There were forty and two children torn. Where have we seen that particular number in Scripture before? The Bible says in Matthew 1:17 "So all the generations from Abraham to David *are* fourteen generations; and from David until the carrying away into Babylon *are* fourteen generations; and from the carrying away into Babylon unto Christ *are* fourteen generations." That is a total of 42 generations. However, if we calculate the generations from Abraham to Jesus listed in Matthew Chapter 1, there are 41. The 42$^{nd}$ generation is a spiritual one; therefore, there must be a people out there pretending to be that generation, but they are not. Wake up slumbering saints! Plainly stated, there is the false church, and there is the Spiritual Bride of Christ. True ministry like Elisha's exposes all that is not of God.

A final note is that the word *children* used in 2 kings 2:24 is a different word than used in 2 Kings 2:23. In verse 23 the word for *children* is the Hebrew word *na'ar* meaning a boy, lad, servant, youth. The word for *children* used in verse 24 is the Hebrew word *yeled* meaning progeny, indicating a son, offspring or one begotten. What a difference! In Christ we are sons of God! He who is born of God sins not; but he that is begotten of God keeps himself, and that wicked one touches him not (1 John 5:18).

From Bethel Elisha went to Carmel meaning a garden or fruitful land and on to Samaria meaning a watch mountain which was Elisha's home. Our ministry powered by the Holy Spirit will take us to wonderful positions of victory and blessing but most of all, rest. There we can experience times of refreshing from God's Presence and watch and pray as commanded. True prophets are rejoicing and hopefully, encouraged to continue to walk in the Spirit. Never get weary in well doing. Prayers are going forth for you fervently from this writer and from Jesus Christ our Lord.

*In them is fulfilled the prophecy of Isaiah: "'You will be ever hearing but never understanding; you will be ever seeing but never perceiving.*
*Matthew 13:14, NIV*

# CHAPTER 5

## SUPERNATURAL WATER

Moab rebelled against Jehoram of Israel in Samaria, and he enlisted the aid of Jehoshaphat king of Judah and the king of Edom. Jehoram worried that they all would be delivered in the hand of Moab, but Jehoshaphat sought for a prophet of God for instruction. One of the servants of the king of Israel noted Elisha who had ministered to Elijah. Jehoshaphat acknowledged that the word of the Lord was with Elisha, and the three kings went to Elisha. Because Elisha regarded only Jehoshaphat, he inquired of the Lord for them.

Notice the methods of Elisha. There is no hocus pocus with him but all things of Eternal Life. Elisha asked for a minstrel to be brought to him. What could the playing on a stringed instrument possibly afford? I noticed a remarkable thing when studying the word minstrel. What the minstrel is and what it does is the same word. The minstrel plays! Stated another way regarding ministry, the Spirit-filled minister and what he does by the Spirit are both the same. In short, the messenger and his Message are one. When that Spiritual Duo is in action, the Supernatural is experienced. Just as the evil spirit left Saul when David played, the Power of God is in full authority. According to the prophet Isaiah, it also speaks of God's readiness to save (38:20). So the minstrel played, and the hand of the Lord came upon Elisha.

Divine instruction then began and God said, Make this valley full of ditches (2 Kings 3:16). As a point of assuring love, the root meaning of ditch is *husbandman*. John 15:1 begins with Jesus declaring, "I am the true vine, and my Father is the husbandman." Just a reminder to reiterate to Whom it all leads. Like Elijah before him whose trench around the altar glorified God (1 Kings 18:35-38), so will the valley full of ditches. Same Divine Demonstration!

The weapons of our warfare are not carnal. God said, without seeing wind or rain the valley would be filled with water for them, their cattle and beasts. With a bonus of blessed assurance, God said it was a light or easy thing to deliver Moab into their hands. God's instructions were very clear. They were to smite every fenced and choice city; fell every good tree; stop all wells of water and mar every good piece of land with stones. If God said it and they believed, it would definitely occur.

Something powerful happened when the meat offering was offered the next morning. Before we see what happened, we need to consider what this particular offering means to God. Remember, this spiritual weapon is mighty through God to the pulling down of strong holds. Since it is not carnal, close scrutiny with spiritual eyes, ears and hearts is a must. Leviticus 2 describes the meat offering which represents Jesus Christ in His human perfections tested by suffering. This offering was an oblation of praise or a gift brought by the worshipper. It speaks to a completely consecrated life. Think on Jesus Who knew no sin, and the essence of this offering will be seen. This is why He was fit to go to the Cross for and as us. This offering consisted of fine flour meaning nothing coarse which blemishes the life; olive oil speaking to the Spirit or anointing; salt pointing to grace, as well as, Covenant; and frankincense indicating worship to God alone. What a weapon! A holy lifestyle.

When this offering was offered, water came by the way of Edom, and the country was filled with water! No wind or rain but an oblation of worship received by God accomplished the same. Hallelujah! The prophet Isaiah prophesied of the vengeance of God upon his enemies. This setting for Elisha's fourth miracle is a microcosm of that eternal Event. All the prophet said was fulfilled in the death, burial and resurrection of Jesus Christ and is still happening in our lives day by day.

Let us listen intently to the Word of God from the prophet Isaiah. "Who *is* this that cometh from Edom, with dyed garments from Bozrah? This *that is* glorious in his apparel, travelling in the greatness of his strength? I that speak in righteousness, mighty to save. Wherefore *art thou* red in thine apparel, and thy garments like him that treadeth in the winefat? I have trodden the winepress alone; and of the people *there was* none with me: for I will tread them in mine anger, and trample them in my fury; and their blood shall be sprinkled upon my garments, and I will stain all my raiment. For the day of vengeance *is* in mine heart, and the year of my redeemed is come. And I looked, and *there was* none to help; and I wondered that *there was* none to uphold: therefore mine own arm brought salvation unto me; and my fury, it upheld me. And I will tread down the people in mine anger, and make them drunk in my fury, and I will bring down their strength to the earth" (Isaiah 63:1-6).

Edom speaks of the flesh or the first Adam. Jesus Christ, the last Adam, brought an end to the earthy man. Jesus alone bore our sins on the Cross. He completely identified with man by becoming sin although He knew no sin. In that sense, He came from Edom. His garments were dyed red stained by the sin of the world. By the way, Bozrah means *sheepfold*. We are His people and the sheep of His pasture (Psalm 100:3). He conquered all by taking our sin and being made righteousness unto us. Prayerfully, we all see that Satan is maximally defeated. If he could just make one think his defeat is future instead of right now, he keeps his foothold in that life. Satan was defeated at the Cross! Vengeance belongs to God and has been exacted in the Cross of Christ.

The Moabites responded in their only known way by taking up their carnal armor. The Power of God causes the enemy to see a form of Christ in Redemption. When the sun shined on the water and it was red, the Moabites thought the water was blood and the kings had killed each other. The red water was reflecting Redemption! Thinking they were rapidly advancing to take the spoils, they went directly into a trap. Israel successfully carried out every command of God to destroy them. We must understand that the Moabites speak to flesh intensified. Moab was the incestuous son of Lot, and when flesh begets flesh, there is nothing spiritual in it. When dealing with flesh, there will always be war with the spirit.

*We have different gifts, according to the grace given to each of us. If your gift is prophesying, then prophesy in accordance with your faith;*

*Romans 12:6, NIV*

# CHAPTER 6

❦

## OIL FOR A WIDOW

There was a woman who was a widow of one of the sons of the prophets. Upon his death, a creditor came to take her two sons for slaves. She explained her situation to Elisha, and he asked her two simple questions. Always remember them. The first question was, "What shall I do for thee?" and the second was, "What hast thou in thine house?" The term widow alone means *deficit*, and the possibility of being without her sons made the situation quite bleak. The only thing she had in her whole house was the very thing she needed. Always remember that, too.

Widows are special to God. He commanded in Exodus 22:22 that no one should afflict a widow or fatherless child. This family was on God's Radar. In spite of the lack that appeared on the surface, any single thing that has spiritual significance is always more than enough. She happened to have had a pot of oil. Only a flask or small oil jug, but it also means *anointing*! There is nothing small about a thing that speaks to the anointing of God. Oil also speaks to the Spirit, and as we see and will continue to see, God's Spirit puts the situation on higher ground.

Having the spiritual "thing" requires faith to bring its fullness into manifestation. God will provided instructions on what is to be done, and all we need to do is obey. Elisha told her to go and borrow empty vessels of all her neighbors. The word vessel has a root meaning *to accomplish* or *finish*. As Jesus said, "It is finished (John 19:30)." What was about to happen to the oil in her small jug could only go into empty vessels. That said, the oil speaking to the Anointing or Jesus would be the preeminent thing therein. No vessels with something already in them are allowed. There is never room for anything else! Got it? Borrow not a few!

The instructions were then to come in, shut the door upon herself and her sons, and pour out into all those vessels and set aside that which is full. To shut the door figuratively means to surrender. Self has no part in this matter. This situation has to be fully placed in God's Hands. One carnal interruption brings all to a screeching halt! This is not the time for one to hesitate to try and figure out what it is that God is doing. Rather, it is time to move in obedience to God with all the heart.

To *set aside* the vessels when full is a term worth investigating. It is no small thing that to *set aside* also means to *pull up and move out on a journey*. If one can only see that every act of obedience toward God is moving us along on our spiritual journey. Such ground is being gained while simultaneously ascending. Imagine the excitement of partaking of the supernatural Power of the Living God. He does not abruptly quit. We can trust Him until the end. As long as there is an empty vessel, the oil will flow. The widow obeyed, her sons brought the vessels to her, and she poured the oil. This continued until all the vessels were full and then and only then, the oil stopped. One will never exhaust the Supply of our God.

She came to Elisha with a good report. She went from being a slave to a lender to one who prospered in the provision of God. From perceived deficiency to the all-sufficiency of God. As a result of her obedient faith, there was plenty of oil to sell and pay the debt, and she had enough for herself and children to live on. Her victory signals the spiritual blessings of heavenly places found in Christ that we should be enjoying (Ephesians 1:3). What a different Economy there is altogether in the Spirit!

Before we leave this miracle, one is reminded that this widow was the wife of a son of the prophets. A son walking in the fullness of the Spirit would have been a priest over his house, and there would have been no creditor involved. This son of the prophet had to know the consequences of debt. We owe no man nothing but to love him, and this dire situation was a result of spiritual neglect. Like him, many carnal ministers are leaving people in a situation where they are forced to deal with a "creditor." Week after week they are placed in dire straits.

The term creditor includes usury which does not please God either. When people hear a message and leave feeling that they owe something, they have been failed. This happens every time Law is ministered or an attempt is made to mix it with grace. One is left a debtor to the whole Law. Such a one then is fallen from grace, and Christ is of no effect to him. Christ is to be ministered in every house by His Spirit. People will then learn love and will walk in the meaning of Romans 13:8 which says if we love one another, we have fulfilled the law. Love is all we owe!

*Follow the way of love and eagerly desire gifts of the Spirit, especially prophecy.*
*1 Corinthians 14:1, NIV*

# CHAPTER 7

## THE GIFT OF A SON

One day Elisha passed through a place called Shunem. What a place of refreshing for it means *double resting place*! A prominent or wealthy woman lived there, and she persuaded him to eat bread or take refreshment. He often passed by there, and because of her hospitality, he stopped to eat with her. She perceived that Elisha was a holy man of God and entreated her husband to make a special chamber for him on the wall. This chamber signifies an upper chamber. The lodging was very accommodating and included a bed, a table, stool and candlestick. What was provided was an expression of Shunem. There was a bed or place to rest while sleeping, a table of place to eat, a stool or place to rest while awake, and a candle for continual light. Decidedly, a double resting place!

Her actions were noted as no "little amount of care" by Elisha. What she did was no ordinary hospitality though good that may be. Her actions carried more weight meaning she acted with reverential fear in taking care of Elisha. Her actions expressed the full meaning of the place she was from, a double resting place. Unlike this woman, many ministries neglect to manifest what they claim to represent. For example, an assembly may call themselves "Church of Love" but one may not experience love at all there. This Shunammite is a wonderful example indeed. Spiritually it looks like this. That which is born of flesh is flesh and that which is born of Spirit is spirit (John 3:6). Flesh in itself is incapable of demonstrating the love of God.

This woman recognized Elisha as someone holy and of God and gave him respect commensurate with that perception. Notice Elisha never demanded anything. He did not even expect anything. His godly character spoke for itself and that is all that is necessary. No unwritten codes of manipulation. He was simply being holy because God is holy.

One day Elisha asked his servant to summon the woman and ask her what she would like in light of all the care shown them. Humbly she came and stood in the entrance to his chamber. He wondered if there was an offer to be spoken for to the king or the captain of the host on her behalf. She simply answered, "I dwell among my own people." Her humility reflected the words of 1 Thessalonians 5:18, which says, "In everything give thanks: for this is the will of God in Christ Jesus concerning you."

Before us is a pure heart. Many would have jumped at the chance to be spoken of to the king or even the captain of the host even though God has already blessed them, and they already enjoy prominence. For such, there is never enough. Oh the "credibility" it adds for some to know people in high places whether they represent the Kingdom of God or not. The only name-dropping that will ever matter is the Name of Jesus! This woman's heart is only toward God and knows no man can provide what she truly seeks but God alone. Do not be ready to sell out so soon! God has some better thing for us!

When Elisha asked his servant what should be done for this woman, the servant noted she had no child, and her husband was old. Elisha called her again and she came. The prophet then prophesied saying, "About this season, according to the time of life, thou shalt embrace a son." The woman was so astounded by the prophecy, she implored Elisha not to lie to her. She was not being disrespectful, but the saying was more than she could comprehend at the moment. To be so greatly impressed by God is overwhelming. In such an instant, one's faculties become frayed as he or she is momentarily held in abeyance by awe. At sudden release, their response flows from a mind unable to comprehend that with which it has been inundated. True prophecy comes to pass, and the woman conceived, and had a son at the very season Elisha said.

The child grew up and went out to his father among the reapers one day. Note the time is that of harvest. He complained to his father saying, "My head, my head!" Could this have been a cry of his spirit to his earthly father that he longed for his Heavenly Father? Remember the sons of the prophets kept reminding Elisha that his master would be taken from *his head*.

The father had his son taken to his mother where he sat on her knees until noon and died. The woman then moved in faith and took her son and laid him on the bed prepared for Elisha, shut the door and went out. Elisha's bed now spoke of *the* resting place instead of *a* resting place. She is moving in the Spirit, and we must see it! There was something so holy about Elisha that even the place he slept was different. There was power there. By shutting the door, as we saw in the last chapter, she surrendered her son to the Power and Authority of the God of Elisha.

Next, she called her husband and requested one of the servants and one of the asses to "run" to the man of God and come back. It is not written that she told her husband of the son's death; therefore he wondered what special occasion required a visit to the man of God. What could it be since there was no special observance such as new moon or Sabbath? Such occasions required offerings unto the Lord according to Israel's Law. What speaks to the fulfillment of the offerings was about to be demonstrated in a most holy manner. When moving in the Spirit, the only day that really matters is the Day of the Lord. The Power of the Cross is in full operation on that Day! Because she moved by faith in the Spirit, she replied, "It shall be well."

The woman went to Elisha at Carmel who saw her afar off. Just as with the Prodigal Son, the Father sees us from afar. Elisha sent his servant to meet her who asked if it was well with her, her husband and her child. Even though the son was physically dead, she answered, "It is well!" She poured her emotions out when speaking to Elisha. Elisha noted her soul was bitter, and she was dealing with something the Lord had hidden from him and not told him.

Elisha gave instructions to his servant to go lay his (Elisha's) staff upon the face of the child. The woman stayed with Elisha. Hopefully, a parallel is being seen between what this woman is now doing by refusing to leave Elisha, and how he refused to leave Elijah. Oh, there is something most different about the True that grips one, and the wise recognize it. Interestingly, Elisha followed her.

Elisha's servant obeyed his instructions and put Elisha's staff on the child's face, but the child did not respond. Specifically, the Scripture says there was neither voice nor hearing. The servant reported to Elisha and when Elisha arrived, the child was dead and lying on his bed. Elisha went in, shut the door with no one but himself and the child and prayed to the Lord. Read carefully the words of 2 Kings 4:34-35 as the miraculous unfolds. "And he went up, and lay upon the child, and put his mouth upon his mouth, and his eyes upon his eyes, and his hands upon his hands: and he stretched himself upon the child; and the flesh of the child waxed warm. Then he returned, and walked in the house to and fro; and went up, and stretched himself upon him: and the child sneezed seven times, and the child opened his eyes."

Would "prophetic" ministry know how to respond in such a situation today? What do the actions of Elisha convey spiritually? From the heavenly perspective, this dead child is being conformed to the Image of Christ and as such must rise. Elisha's mouth upon his mouth. He is being spiritually enabled to declare what God says. Elisha's eyes upon his eyes! His sight will be by the Spirit or that which truly matters. Elisha's hands upon his hands. The consecrated works Jesus did, we will do and greater! Elisha stretched himself upon the child who then became warm indicating a response to Resurrection Life within?

Dear prophet and all God's beloved, are you causing someone to grow up into the measure of Christ's fullness, or are you prancing about before a Lifeless group? It is time to walk to and fro in the house, the Lord's House, in the Power of the Spirit until every square inch is permeated with His glory. Go back and stretch Christ over His people until the spiritually dead children in your midst sneeze seven times.

The root meaning of the word *sneeze* is to become a stranger. Seven speaks to spiritual perfection. This son is now risen to Life Eternal in Christ. He will now be able to understand that because he is alive in the spirit, this world is no longer home, and he is a stranger here! That is why the Apostle Peter implored his hearers by saying, "Dearly beloved, I beseech you as strangers and pilgrims, abstain from fleshly lusts, which war against the soul (1 Peter 2:11)." We are a people inhabiting the spiritual realm by faith and only sojourning in the earth.

Perhaps the similarity between the miracle of Elijah presenting a son alive and Elisha's comes to mind. To refresh we will review Elijah's response in the face of death and see what we may learn. 1 Kings 17:18-20 gives the account of the widow's conversation with Elijah concerning the sickness and death of her son as well as his prayer to God. It reads, "And she said to Elijah, What have you against me, O man of God? Have you come to me to call my sin to remembrance and to slay my son? He said to her, Give me your son. And he took him from her bosom and carried him up into the chamber where he stayed and laid him upon his own bed. And Elijah cried to the Lord and said, O Lord my God, have You brought further evil (calamity) upon the widow with whom I sojourn, by slaying her son? And he stretched himself upon the child three times, and cried unto the LORD, and said, O LORD my God, I pray thee, let this child's soul come into him again."

Let us peek at a truth that may be easily overlooked. Notice both Elijah and Elisha were baffled at the death of these sons. Elisha even commented that God had kept the thing from him, and we have just seen Elijah's query in his prayer to God indicating he did not fully understand what was happening. Allow the following Scriptures to illuminate our thinking. In Acts 4, Peter is preaching to the Sanhedrin. He said in verse 10, "Be it known unto you all, and to all the people of Israel, that by the name of Jesus Christ of Nazareth, whom ye crucified, whom God raised from the dead, even by him doth this man stand here before you whole." Romans 10:9 states, "That if thou shalt confess with thy mouth the Lord Jesus, and shalt believe in thine heart that God hath raised him from the dead, thou shalt be saved. God is a Spirit and Romans 8:11 says, "But if the Spirit of him that raised up Jesus from the dead dwell in you, he that raised up Christ from the dead shall also quicken your mortal bodies by his Spirit that dwells in you."

In case we did not see the Supreme Ability that is God's alone, this is the precise point being driven home now. What these deaths speak to is between a son and God alone. Prophets are vessels and not God Himself. Only God has the Power, but He sure loves to express Himself through pure vessels! How we should all yearn to be such unto Him. Our duty is to express Him as He flows so mightily in us. In the Book of Revelation, John kept meeting messengers and wanted to worship them. He had to be warned not to. That is because in the Spirit, everything should be fully representative of God alone. Good job, Elijah and Elisha!

Still visiting the miracle of Elijah, regard the fact that a change of possession and position must take place in order for Resurrection Life to manifest. The widow's son had to be handed over to Elijah and moved to Elijah's space in the house. He had to be laid on Elijah's bed (bier), picturing our being made conformable to Jesus' death (Philippians 3:10). Elijah prayed but did not call sin into remembrance. We have an Advocate with the Father (1 John 2:1). Elijah's faith with works was demonstrated as he stretched himself upon the child three times. In other words, he made the son's situation conform fully to the Redemptive Work of Christ. Elijah stretched or *measured* himself in all three realms (spirit, soul and body) of this son indicating a complete work in righteousness. He then simply asked God to let the child's soul come into him again. God answered. The result was a son presented alive. The result of true ministry of the Word will always be a son presented alive!

*Then he said to me, Prophesy to the breath; prophesy, son of man, and say to it, 'This is what the Sovereign Lord says: Come, breath, from the four winds and breathe into these slain, that they may live.'*

*Ezekiel 37:9, NIV*

# CHAPTER 8

### POISON POTTAGE

Elisha came to Gilgal. As noted earlier, Gilgal speaks of the place where the reproach of Egypt or bondage to the world system was rolled away. There was a famine in the land. Food was scarce and today this situation has a two-fold meaning. Not only is food or the Word scarce, there is also a famine of hearing the words of the Lord as noted by the prophet Amos (8:11). There is want, even destitution in some places. The Bread of Life is prevalent, but many choose spiritual starvation because of their love of the world more than the Lord. How did a true prophet respond to this state of affairs? Let us see.

With the sons of the prophets seated before him, Elisha told his servant to set on a great pot and seethe pottage for them. One of them went out into the field to gather herbs. We know the field represents the world because Jesus said so when teaching a parable of the tares of the field (Matthew 13:38). While the person was gathering herbs, he found a wild vine and gathered a lap full of wild gourds. Let us pause and carefully note every event in association with the upcoming miracle.

For us today, we know that Jesus is the true Vine. We are His branches. The Substance that flows from Him causes us to bear spiritual fruit. Is it not amazing that today one would still gather from a wild vine instead of the True? If the vine is wild so is the fruit. To rid ministries of the overbearing chaos of the wild man and his carnal nature, get rid of the wild vine and call upon Christ, the True Vine.

Many need to examine what is being ingested spiritually. What is being cooked up in our ministries? Will it being life or death?

A lap full of gourds. The Hebrew word for lap also means *to act* or *deal treacherously or faithlessly*. These gourds were shredded into the pot, and the sons of the prophet did not know what they were. Unlike the God-sent manna which means *what is it?* these gourds are not from heaven! With the manna came Divine instruction. This act is a classic example of someone preaching something because someone else said it, and it has not been Spirit-verified. Think about some of the things being dished out in ministry today. Is it a wild thing from the world or a heaven-sent sure word of prophecy?

So they served up the pottage, found they could not eat it, and told Elisha there was death in the pot. Death! Something in the pot could kill. Sounds much like the Law. We have been made able ministers of the New Testament; not of the letter, but of the spirit: for the letter kills, but the spirit gives life (2 Corinthians 3:6). If one would reflect on the last service attended from start to finish, it is highly likely that the letter was ministered, and there was death in the pot. This is most serious and extremely dangerous!

Praise God for Elisha and all that he speaks to. The very Spirit of the Living Christ will help us in such situations. He knows exactly what to do. Death, where is your sting? The solution was to bring meal. Meal is that which has been ground or pulverized. It is that which speaks to humility in its most intense meaning. Jesus thought it not robbery to be equal with God, but took on the form of a Servant. There is no humility greater than His. He died for the sin of the world although He knew no sin. The Law which is the strength of sin was fulfilled by Christ Jesus. What pictures sin was dealt with in that pot! Cast meal or Christ into the pot, pour Him out and the people can eat. God's Spirit was poured out at Pentecost, not death cooked up by man.

Once that which speaks to Christ is put in our spiritual food, there will be no harm in the pot. The word harm is jolting! Two Hebrew words are used to define it. One word is *speech* and the other is *evil*. It literally renders, there was no evil speech or utterance in the pot! Merciful Jesus! People must be fed from that which does not cause hurt and is not grievous. Ephesians 4:31 warns us to get rid of all bitterness, rage and anger, brawling and evil speaking, along with every form of malice. These poisonous things are in pots which brew many carnal sermons.

A further look at speech can be seen from Psalm 12:2 which reads, "They speak vanity every one with his neighbor: [with] flattering lips [and] with a double heart do they speak." Speech indeed betrays a person, especially when evil attempts to feign goodness. As our Lord stated in Luke 6:45, "...an evil man out of the evil treasure of his heart brings forth that which is evil: for out of the abundance of the heart his mouth speaks." Sadly, oppressive speech is prevalent today and often spewed under the guise of ministerial instruction.

Believers are cautioned to listen intently for the Spirit's Voice in order to avoid the seducing words of the oppressor that lead to death. As seen above in Psalm 12:2, the words of the oppressor have three distinct characteristics. They are vanity meaning empty. Empty words cannot produce spiritual understanding that brings forth the wisdom of Christ Jesus. The giveaway sign of emptiness is that it is not Christ-centered. Emptiness places temporal interests at its center. It can only appease the carnal nature leaving a spiritually thirsty heart stranded in dryness and weariness.

The second characteristic is the smooth talk of flattering lips. The insincere heart seeks to feel good while dodging accountability. Deep down one can know change is required to make spiritual progress, but instead postpones it. Foolish! While seeking to feel better about delaying spiritual progress and deferring to carnal lusts, one is content with a messenger with flattering lips. Instead of growing up into maturity in Christ, one is content to be pacified again and again in the fallen state of the unregenerate man.

Lastly, the oppressor's words are characterized by double talk. A double heart speaks of a double mind which renders the message unstable. One cannot serve God and mammon, yet one futile attempt after another is made to try it. Such oppressive speech is laid bare in that of the beast described in the Revelation Chapter

13:11, "And I beheld another beast coming up out of the earth; and he had two horns like a lamb, and he spoke as a dragon." When seen through eyes of the Spirit, the wickedness of the oppressor's double talk is fully exposed. The messenger deceives by trying to appear to represent the Anointed One (*horns of a lamb*); however, the speech is that of the dragon, the Wicked One (*he spoke as a dragon*). "If any have an ear, let him hear." When all else fails and it will, go back to the Divine Basic of Love, Christ Jesus our Lord. For this is the love of God, that we keep His commandments: and His commandments are not grievous (1 John 5:3).

*If I have the gift of prophecy and can fathom all mysteries and all knowledge, and if I have a faith that can move mountains, but do not have love, I am nothing.*
*1 Corinthians 13:2, NIV*

# CHAPTER 9

## *MULTIPLICATION OF BREAD*

A man came from Baalshalisha which means *thrice-great God*. He is not mentioned by name, but he brought Elisha the bread of the firstfruits. Before proceeding, the importance of firstfruits to God must be carefully weighed. Firstfruits mean the first in place time order or rank. It is the beginning or chief thing. Related words in Scripture are first, firstborn, first begotten, and first ripe. In Exodus 23:19, it was commanded the first of the firstfruits of their land be brought into the house of the LORD their God.

So we begin with a God-honoring action on the part of one who is from a place that ascribes greatness to the Godhead. This man brought twenty loaves of barley and full ears of corn in the husk to Elisha. Both items speak powerfully to Christ in Glory. Beginning with barley which speaks to resurrection, one may recall the story of Ruth who came to Boaz's field during the time of barley harvest. Like Boaz to Ruth, Christ Jesus is our Kinsman Redeemer. Just as Jesus multiplied barley loaves, they are multiplied in this miracle of Elisha.

Now is a great time to review Jesus's miracle to see a heavenly pattern of what it all looks like in Spirit-led ministry. In John Chapter 6, there was a lad with five barley loaves and two small fish. More than enough for a lad but not nearly enough for a multitude of about 5,000 without supernatural and Divine Intervention. Jesus simply instructed all to sit down. It is important to learn that the Power of God is experienced from a position of rest. Let us all go sit down or rest and allow Jesus to minister! Jesus gave thanks and distributed bread and fish until all were filled and twelve baskets of fragments of the barley loaves remained. As a reminder, twelve is the Bible number for government, and God's government can do many things that man's government finds impossible.

Now let us observe what Elisha did with the firstfruits. Always take into account that Elisha's ministry points to what we should be experiencing in ministry today because Jesus went to Father. This point is a thread of truth continually woven throughout this book because of its supreme importance. The man gave Elisha the firstfruits, and he said to give them to the people to eat. 1 Corinthians 15:20 reads, "But now is Christ risen from the dead, *and* become the firstfruits of them that slept." See the endless reasons why Jesus must be ministered to His people?

Elisha's servant noted there were a hundred men, yet Elisha repeated his instructions to give to the people so they could eat. God then spoke by Elisha and said they would eat and leave thereof. Returning to a previous point, obedience is very vital in accessing the benefits of the Kingdom and Power of God. Once the servant set the food before the people, they ate and left some as God said.

*Now to him who is able to establish you in accordance with my gospel, the message I proclaim about Jesus Christ, in keeping with the revelation of the mystery hidden for long ages past, but now revealed and made known through the prophetic writings by the command of the eternal God, so that all the Gentiles might come to the obedience that comes from faith. To the only wise God be glory forever through Jesus Christ! Amen.*

*Romans 16:25-27, NIV*

# CHAPTER 10

## THE HEALING OF NAAMAN

Naaman was a captain of the Syrian army with considerable influence with the king of Syria. Despite his status, he was a leper. Leprosy is disease of the skin or "covering" and symbolizes sin. Naaman is an example of anyone who lives apart from Christ Jesus our Lord and Savior. Christ is our "covering" of Light wherein no sin abides. Because of a captured maid from Israel who served Naaman's wife, he would experience healing. The reader is highly encouraged to read 2 Kings Chapter 5.

Although captive, the maid remembered her people and her God's ability through His prophet. She knew that God could recover Naaman of leprosy. Unable to help him and in response to the maid's suggestion, the king of Syria sent a letter with Naaman to the king of Israel to recover him of his leprosy. A great bounty of "ten talents of silver, and six thousand [pieces] of gold, and ten changes of raiment" accompanied Naaman as compensation. The numbers "ten" and "six" are a telltale indication of the only means by which the carnal man learns and has his understanding, and above all, operates. Ten meaning Law or letter that kills and six meaning the number of man are the emblems of carnality. Nothing spiritually distinguishing whatsoever! Silver speaks of redemption and gold of our Divine nature in Christ. Kindly note the mixture of spiritual and carnal which is the calling card of the Harlot.

To recover means *to gather together and take away*. Jesus Christ recovered us fully when He gathered us into Himself and bore our sin away on the Cross. Jesus is quoted in John 12:32 saying, "And I, if I be lifted up from the earth, will draw all [men] unto me." The price for Naaman's leprosy was paid from the foundation of the world, making him a wonderful example for our learning as the redeemed of the Lord. Grace is priceless and cannot be bought.

Upon receipt of the letter from the king of Syria, the king of Israel responded in a way that reveals man's helplessness to deal with what speaks to sin. 2 Kings 5:7 reads, "And it came to pass, when the king of Israel had read the letter, that he rent his clothes, and said, Am I God, to kill and to make alive, that this man doth send unto me to recover a man of his leprosy?" How the precious Gospel of Jesus Christ, His death, burial and resurrection ring out and come alive even in the king's words of utmost inadequacy

"From that time forth began Jesus to shew unto his disciples, how that he must go unto Jerusalem, and suffer many things of the elders and chief priests and scribes, and <u>be killed, and be raised again the third day</u> (Matthew 16:21)." "<u>I [am] he that liveth, and was dead</u>; and, behold, <u>I am alive for evermore</u>, Amen; and have the keys of hell and of death (Revelation 1:18)." "And unto the angel of the church in Smyrna write; These things saith the first and the last, <u>which was dead, and is alive</u> (Revelation 2:8)." This king was keenly aware that only the True God of Israel was able to grant the king of Syria's request. Well, here is presented a case of one kingdom of this world that could not stand against the Kingdom of God. To heal leprosy, which we know speaks to sin, requires an act that exemplifies the death, burial, and resurrection of a Sinless Sacrifice! Glory to God and Father of our Lord Jesus Christ.

When Elisha heard that the king of Israel rent his clothes, he enquired and responded, "Let him come now to me, and he shall know that there is a prophet in Israel." A true prophet is one who speaks by Divine Power. Like Jesus, such a prophet speaks or declares only what he hears from God. Today, we are blessed to be joint heirs with Christ. There is a living ministry because God's Word was accomplished in Christ Jesus Who did not return void to Father. Divine expression is alive! That is why there is such power unto salvation in the preaching of the Cross. Salvation's power is encrypted in the Gospel. When something is encrypted, it is encoded to prevent unauthorized access. Praise God for the tamper-free power of salvation which is authorized by the Spirit when the true Gospel is preached. One thing that is certain is that hirelings and false prophets will not be able to hack into the Power of God.

Elisha sent a messenger to Naaman with simple instructions, "Go and wash in Jordan seven times, and thy flesh shall come again to thee, and thou shalt be clean." Because Elisha did not personally respond to Naaman and his entourage, Naaman became offended. Oh that we could see the power inherent in the message! The Word is the Life and Power! To become "clean" requires baptism into His death. Elisha sent Naaman the Eternal Formula for becoming ceremonially clean or pure.

His instructions give a prominent exhibition of what happens at Redemption. *Seven* speaks to spiritual perfection or completion. Why wash in Jordan? An enraged Naaman demanded to know its significance and preference over rivers in Damascus. Jordan means *to descend*, and it is a perfect picture of complete immersion or baptism into Christ. "For as many of you as have been baptized into Christ have put on Christ" (Galatians 3:27).

God's grace is determined to see us through to the benefits of our recovery. There were encouraging servants with Naaman who convinced him to follow Elisha's instructions. Elisha's message reflected the simplicity in Christ Jesus. It did not contain all the gobbledygook of man's carnal ordinances and religious traditions. No need for a bunch of classes from sons of the prophets. Simply believe then do that which speaks to identification with the Cross of Christ. Naaman washed and was cleansed. His servants recognized there was no greater thing to be done than those simple steps bidden by the prophet. Before receiving the victory, Naaman had a mindset atypical of unbelievers and some believers alike, today. For some, there is a preconceived manner as to how God is supposed to work. Many confess Ephesians 2:8-9 where we find our salvation is not of works but grace, then unwittingly forget about grace and replace it with religious works of man's hands. Naaman's first error was, "I thought," indicating leaning to one's own understanding instead of full reliance upon God.

With careful reading of Leviticus Chapter 14, we find the law of the cleansing of the leper. It is evident by Naaman's remarks that he had heard aspects of the letter of the Law. He said, "Behold, I thought, He will surely come out to me, and stand, and call on the name of the LORD his God, and strike his hand over the place, and recover the leper." There are five specific things that Naaman thought should have happened. Five is the number of grace. Law and error create a dam in the flow of grace into a person's life. Like Naaman, many know part of the letter which kills but have no ability to discern the spirit of the Word which gives life. Christ has fulfilled the Law and condemned sin in the flesh "that the righteousness of the law might be fulfilled in us, who walk not after the flesh, but after the Spirit" (Romans 8:4).

"And he returned to the man of God, he and all his company, and came, and stood before him: and he said, Behold, now I know that [there is] no God in all the earth, but in Israel: now therefore, I pray thee, take a blessing of thy servant (2 Kings 5:15)." Earlier Naaman had expected that Elisha should have stood before him and all his company. Now he has the correct approach! It is paramount to be ever mindful that what Elisha speaks to spiritually as Israel's Prophet is a type of Christ Jesus's ministry in resurrection power. This point will be repeated numerous times in this book. In other words, He does not stand before us, but rather, we stand before Him!

Naaman's heart was to bless the prophet of God. Elisha further represents the love of God, and His saving grace for which there is no fee. Elisha refused reward. The ministry of grace always gives proof that it is more blessed to give than to receive. Such grace has all sufficiency in Christ. There is an eternal government of spiritual perfection wrought within this grace, and it becomes replenished immediately as it blesses.

"And Naaman said, Shall there not then, I pray thee, be given to thy servant two mules' burden of earth? for thy servant will henceforth offer neither burnt offering nor sacrifice unto other gods, but unto the LORD (II Kings 5:17)." This verse signals the new heart of Naaman as a result of his recovery from his leprosy. Its meaning is so robust and will hopefully cause a heart-check for every reader. Of all the things he could ask, why *two mules' burden of earth*. Perhaps a glance at Exodus Chapter 20:22-26 will give us insight. "And the LORD said unto Moses, Thus thou shalt say unto the children of Israel, Ye have seen that I have talked with you from heaven. Ye shall not make with me gods of silver, neither shall ye make unto you gods of gold. An altar of earth thou shalt make unto me, and shalt sacrifice thereon thy burnt offerings, and thy peace offerings, thy sheep, and thine oxen: in all places where I record my name I will come unto thee, and I will bless thee."

The earth was likely for an altar. Naaman now fully realized that the only true God is the God of Israel. He could now have a place to meet God. Although he still had to accompany his master into the temple of his master's pagan god, Naaman, himself, would worship God in the manner He ordained. The parting words between Naaman and Elisha were, "Go in peace." As believers, our earthly temples belong to Christ, and He bids us the same, "Peace I leave with you, my peace I give unto you: not as the world giveth, give I unto you. Let not your heart be troubled, neither let it be afraid."

*For prophecy never had its origin in the human will, but prophets, though human, spoke from God as they were carried along by the Holy Spirit.*
*2 Peter 1:19-21, NIV*

# CHAPTER 11

## GEHAZI IS SMITTEN WITH LEPROSY

This account will clearly show the pure in heart, as well as, those who are not, that there is no such thing as "payment" for the Spiritual blessings of God. Why is there all the collecting of worldly things and merchandizing in return for what should be Spirit-led ministry in the Church today? As Isaiah 55:1 declares, "Come, all you who are thirsty, come to the waters; and you who have no money, come, buy and eat! Come, buy wine and milk without money and without cost." Water, milk and wine speak to the Word and the Spirit thereof. The Word became Flesh, and He is the Healer. The Spirit of the Word effects spiritual things such as the healing of Naaman. Be ever, ever cognizant that Elisha is Gehazi's master, and his ministry is not ordinary. Today, it is the Spirit of Truth Himself ministering through people. In the simplest terms, it is most holy and nothing to be handled in a devious manner.

As Naaman was leaving, Gehazi, the servant of Elisha, followed him and took of the items sent by the Syrian king. His error is a blaring signal to those seeking material gain (*filthy lucre*) under false pretense of the "Master's request" or outright fleecing and lying to the people of God. Is it worth taking on the unnecessary evil of it all? God's Word is stable and changes not. It is forever settled in heaven. As Elisha's heart or his inner man or spirit went with Gehazi, so does the Spirit of God with His servants.

Elisha asked Gehazi a direct question, "Is it a time to receive money, and to receive garments, and olive yards, and vineyards, and sheep, and oxen, and menservants, and maidservants?" This is still a valid question today! One may be unreservedly certain that the spiritual counterparts to the natural things just named are being traded off at an alarming rate. Sadly, that tradeoff looks like so: redemption for money; being clothed upon with Christ for garments; the anointing for olive yards; the Spirit's Power for vineyards; a living sacrifice holy and acceptable unto God for sheep and oxen; and sons and daughters living in total victory for men and maidservants. It is absolutely not worth it!

Up to this point Gehazi seemed reputable. His plight shows what each person will be faced with in this world: the lust of the flesh, the lust of the eyes, and the pride of life. If we feed on the Lord Jesus Christ, we will know to choose what is good and refuse evil. If we feed on mixture, an inescapable snare awaits. Those who are wise in their own strength should be extra careful here. Just as Jesus was tempted by the devil, whose method of operating is in the aforementioned areas of lust and pride, so will we.

We are at a serious time as described in Romans 13:11-14. It is weighty in its declaration, "And that, knowing the time, that now it is high time to awake out of sleep: for now is our salvation nearer than when we believed. The night is far spent, the day is at hand: let us therefore cast off the works of darkness, and let us put on the armor of light. Let us walk honestly, as in the day; not in rioting and drunkenness, not in chambering and wantonness, not in strife and envying. But put ye on the Lord Jesus Christ, and make not provision for the flesh, to fulfil the lusts thereof."

Gehazi's name means *valley of vision*. We may then say he represents a visionary. There are countless visionaries today with elaborate and exorbitant schemes to bring glory only to themselves. The Church is merely a resourceful means of exploitation for them. If such a goal is deep rooted in the heart, one can go for years appearing to be a faithful servant, yet the heart will be filled with lust while steadily growing evil. At some point God and mammon will face off, and make no mistake about it, God will win.

Of what benefit is it? The whole thing began with a lie that Gehazi was acting on the word of his master, Elisha. Secondly, it was under the pretense that is was for two young men of the sons of the prophets. Then Gehazi asked for a talent of silver and two changes of garments. Think for a moment! How would he have accounted for these gifts while serving Elisha? How are hirelings today accounting for all they have amassed while claiming to serve God? Generous Naaman gave him two talents of silver and two changes of garments and had two of his servants carry them for Gehazi who hid them in a tower. Notice the multiple application of the number two regarding Naaman's gifts. Two speaks to witness. It so evidently sets forth the truth that the one trespassing is not getting away with anything! Foremost, the all-seeing and knowing Spirit of God is aware of every detail. Repent.

With the audacity of a thief in open daylight, Gehazi stood before Elisha, and when asked where he was coming from, denied ever going. The Spirit of God cannot be fooled! Elisha's specific words were, "Went not mine heart *with thee*, when the man turned again from his chariot to meet thee?" Elisha's ministry is such that there is never a time to receive anything associated with this world as payment for obeying God. Temporal does not fit in Spirit, and we must stop trying to force it.

We must not cloud the righteousness of God's judgment with Gehazi's experience. He went out from Elisha as white as snow with leprosy. Leprosy or sin was a condition that openly confessed his nature. He was a sinner. The judgment was that the leprosy of Naaman would cleave to Gehazi and his seed forever. The heartbeat of the matter comes from 1 John 4:2 which tells us every spirit that confesses that Jesus Christ is come in the flesh is of God. This confession is not just lip service but a holy lifestyle. Gehazi's actions did not represent God but sin, and the leprosy made his true confession evident.

Leviticus 13 contains the law of the leper. It states in verse 13 (NIV), "The priest is to examine them, and if the disease has covered their whole body, he shall pronounce them clean. Since it has all turned white, they are clean. One's falling from grace does not nullify the Power of the Cross." Stay focused on the Power of God because over in 2 Kings 8, Gehazi is being used as an instrument in the restoration of the woman whose son was raised from the dead. More is mentioned of him in Chapter 15 of this book. The ways of God pass all understanding. Oh, the love and righteousness of these Kingdom dynamics!

As the Apostle Paul ministered to the Corinthians, we are to run the race so as to win the prize. That means always being guided by the Spirit. We are running for a crown that lasts forever. That is why we do not run aimlessly. Paul wisely used the analogy of a boxer fighting the air. With a right Cross, he stunned them by saying, "I strike a blow to my body and make it my slave so that after I have preached to others, I myself will not be disqualified for the prize." What a strengthening example to run well!

*Then the Lord said to me, "The prophets are prophesying lies in my name. I have not sent them or appointed them or spoken to them. They are prophesying to you false visions, divinations, idolatries and the delusions of their own minds.*

*Jeremiah 14:14, NIV*

# CHAPTER 12

*THE IRON DID SWIM*

Before we consider the twelfth miracle of Elisha which was to recover a borrowed axe, the Spirit is encouraging us to look very hard at the setting first. For convenience, the following Scripture is inserted for the reader.

Scripture: 2 Kings 6: 1-7

1 ***And*** the sons of the prophets said unto Elisha, Behold now, the place where we dwell with thee is too strait for us.

2 ***Let*** us go, we pray thee, unto Jordan, and take thence every man a beam, and let us make us a place there, where we may dwell. And he answered, Go ye.

3 ***And*** one said, Be content, I pray thee, and go with thy servants. And he answered, I will go.

4 ***So*** he went with them. And when they came to Jordan, they cut down wood.

5 ***But*** as one was felling a beam, the axe head fell into the water: and he cried, and said, Alas, master! for it was borrowed.

6 ***And*** the man of God said, Where fell it? And he shewed him the place. And he cut down a stick, and cast it in thither; and the iron did swim.

7 ***Therefore*** said he, Take it up to thee. And he put out his hand, and took it.

Sons of the prophets may also represent believers set apart to minister the testimony of Jesus Christ or the spirit of prophecy (Revelation 19:10). This group is often one to whom, and at times through whom, God also demonstrates Christ's Resurrection Power. Although the scene in the above Scripture has them naturally positioned in a strait place, it speaks to a most powerful position spiritually for all. Since the renewed spirit is mature and the soul (mind, will, and emotions) have to catch up to it, the sons of the prophets did not realize the magnitude of their location and set out to "test the waters." Many believers do that today by not fully realizing our position and power in Christ, and seek to do other exploits in His Holy Name only to come back front and center on Him again.

The sons of the prophets above were in a place that was *too strait* in their minds. A strait place is one that is small or narrow and confining. There is no room to turn to the right or left. All sufficiency in God is found in the strait place, and Jesus described it as a way that leads to life. "Enter ye in at the strait gate: for wide is the gate, and broad is the way that leads to destruction, and many there be which go in there at: Because strait is the gate, and narrow is the way, which leads unto life, and few there be that find it (Matthew 7:13-14)." Christ Jesus is the Way, the Truth and the Life. Hear Him today.

They sought and received Elisha's permission to go unto Jordan to make a larger place to dwell. Jordan means *to descend.* Elisha's ministry foreshadows the ministry of Christ Jesus. It is one that brings life to a situation of death, failure, or defeat. Unlike evil, it is not intrusive, violent and destructive, but instead waits for the bidding of a pure heart. Although they were already situated in a place that speaks to us of a powerful spiritual location, they did not understand and sought to go on their own. The one glimmer of wisdom in their action was inviting the man of God to accompany them.

Certainly, when one is outside the way that leads to life, an instance of failure only deliverable by the ability of God will arise. They went to Jordan and cut down wood to build a dwelling place. One's borrowed axe head fell into the water. *Alas, Master* was a cry of desperation for immediate help. The water, which represents the Word, makes for a powerful place of testing. The circumstances rapidly went downhill, and their attitudes changed from enthusiasm with its sensual appeal to utter despair. An axe head of iron had fallen in the water, out of sight and apparently impossible to retrieve. Elisha now is also a picture of the Helper Himself in the midst. Had they gone without Elisha, a very serious condition would have emerged for which they were all powerless to reverse. May we invite the Holy Spirit to accompany us today and every day!

As seen, the axe head fell into the water while cutting down a tree. "Cutting down" is translated "cut off" in two very interesting Scriptures. They read:

Isaiah 53:8 **He** was taken from prison and from judgment: and who shall declare his generation? for he was cut off out of the land of the living: for the transgression of my people was he stricken.

Lamentations 3:54 **Waters** flowed over mine head; [then] I said, I am cut off.

The axe head is also referred to as "the iron" in the verse 6 above. Iron speaks to the will and strength. Upon closer examination a picture of Redemption surfaces again from this whole situation from start to finish. A living tree (Jesus Christ) was cut down. His will and strength or His essence became one with *the water* or Word of God. They are at Jordan which means *to descend*. To descend further means leaving a high place and to go to a low place. That is precisely what Jesus did. Ephesians 4:9 reminds us, "Now that he ascended, what is it but that he also descended first into the lower parts of the earth?" But, one might ask, how does the term borrowed fit here? Webster defines "borrow" as "to take from another by request and consent, with a view to use the thing taken for a time, and return it." Jesus completed His earthly ministry and is set down at the right hand of the throne of God (Hebrews 12:2). He returned to the Father.

Further, a picture is seen of Christ Jesus fulfilling the Law. God gave a command in the Old Covenant to illustrate a truth for the New. According to Exodus 22:14, "If a man borrowed anything from his neighbor, and it be hurt, or die, its owner not being with it, he shall fully make it good." The wisdom of Christ reveals the importance of the *borrowed* iron. Something borrowed must be returned or made good. To *make it good* includes words and terms such as to make whole, finish, recompense, covenant of peace, complete, all of which are attributes of Christ and His Redemptive Work.

The son of the prophet to whom this experience happened is another picture of a believer who must fully identify with the death, burial and resurrection of Jesus Christ. Once he experienced what spoke to Christ's death and burial, he had to employ Elisha's help (the Power of God) to raise the iron. What returns is in like kind, "For if we have been planted together in the likeness of his death, we shall be also [in the likeness] of [his] resurrection *(Romans 6:5)."* As believers, we often remove ourselves from the experience, but what is true of Christ is also true of us. His death was our death and His life is our life. In Him all have been "made good" and returned to Father.

The submerged iron summons a thought of hope lost. Good news! Christ our hope of glory is within! Elisha also "cut down;" however, the term takes on a different meaning than the action of the son of the prophets. The term "cut down" as used by Elisha means to cut evenly and is only used one other place in Scripture in Song of Solomon 4:2, "Thy teeth [are] like a flock [of sheep that are even] shorn, which came up from the washing; whereof every one bear twins, and none [is] barren among them. Cutting down a stick is compared to shorn sheep, a metaphor for the Bride's teeth. Teeth understandably mean *to sharpen*, but the same Hebrew word for teeth is translated in Deuteronomy 6:7 as *teach diligently*! ("And thou shalt teach them diligently unto thy children..."). God is raising up ministry in the earth today that will teach His people diligently concerning His accomplished Word.

"And he cut down a stick, and cast it in thither..." Upon further spiritual observation of this term *"cut down"* or *"cut off"* referring to Elisha's action, another wonderful truth materializes. As stated, its only other use in Scripture is *"shorn."* When considering a shorn sheep, something is *cut off* from a living creature normally used as a sacrifice. In the shearing process, the creature itself is not depleted in anyway. It perpetually provides or sacrifices a part of itself making it comparable to God's grace. Like grace, a picture of an inexhaustible supply is viewable from this event.

What speaks to the grace resulting from Resurrection Life (a stick cut off a tree of life) was cast into the water or Word and *the iron did swim.* There are very few other uses in Scripture for the Hebrew word translated here *"swim."* One use that will help our understanding is the word *"overflow"* in Deuteronomy 11:4, which rehearses God's greatness toward His people, Israel. "And what he did unto the army of Egypt, unto their horses, and to their chariots; how he made the water of the Red sea to overflow them as they pursued after you, and [how] the LORD hath destroyed them unto this day." God's delivering Power is clearly seen at work as Elisha demonstrated an act comparable to Christ Jesus' obedience in the Finished Work of the Cross. Jesus died and was buried and God raised Him up the third day, and shewed him openly (Acts 10:40). Interestingly, The Companion Bible margin equates the phrase, *"the iron did swim"* as *"made him see the iron."* Praise God, Jesus was shown openly and victorious over death. Believers are too raised in Him in newness of life! We are new creatures in Christ raised up to overcome.

*Together, we are his house, built on the foundation of the apostles and the prophets. And the cornerstone is Christ Jesus himself.*
*Ephesians 2:20, NLT*

# Chapter 13

## The Blind See Naturally and Spiritually

There was again war in the land between the kings of Syria and Israel. Elisha warned the king of Israel who was able to avoid the snare of the Syrians. The Syrian king, ignorant to the Power of God, was certain a traitor was in his midst. No traitor but rather Elisha, a true prophet of God, with Ability to tell the king of Syria's most intimate details. The Syrian king sent to spy on Elisha and to seize him.

Elisha was at Dothan. The Syrian army came by night and encompassed the city. Fearful, Elisha's servant wondered what they would do. Elisha told him not to fear because there were more with them than with the Syrians. This is where it would again be very pathetic to try to see and act by natural means. To pause a moment, ever wonder what a nation would be like whose God is the Lord? A people who truly trust Him without wavering? One would think the history of wars would cause somebody to have a desire to stand in the Power of God alone.

Elisha prayed and asked the Lord to open his servant's eyes. The young man saw and the mountain was full of horses and chariots of fire round about Elisha. What Elisha saw at Elijah's ascension never left him! May that truth shore up a troubled mind during times of fear and loneliness. The very chariots and horses of fire of the Captain of the Lord's host! Do we believe Jesus when He said He will never leave or forsake us? Pray that eyes come wide open in the Spirit. As believers, we are not alone!

Get fully acquainted with the power of prayer. The Syrian army advanced, and Elisha prayed that God would smite them with blindness. God did. Notice from 2 Kings 6:19, Elisha was in full command of the enemy's army, and they followed him to Samaria. Once in Samaria, their eyes were opened. When the king of Israel asked whether he should smite them, Elisha gave him a spiritual education. The king of Israel did not seem to realize that they were actually captives. There was a code of conduct for the treatment of a captive which was to set bread and water before them and send them to their master. In obedience, the king of Israel complied and the bands of Syria did not come to their land anymore.

We saw the miraculous dual side of blindness. The Syrians were smitten with blindness for a time, and Elisha's servant's eyes that were spiritually blind were opened. Notice when blind spiritually, one is oblivious to the Power and Presence of Almighty God. When one is blind naturally, he may be a battle-tested soldier yet helpless to defend himself. Both cases require being led by someone with sight. Elisha had sight in both realms. That which is truly prophetic has the same ability.

Jesus left us with a lesson on blindness in the healing of Bartimaeus that would be wise to insert here. Bartimaeus was the blind son of Timaeus, a name whose root meaning is *unclean*. This offspring of an unclean one is a representative of all who are apart from Christ. His state in spirit, soul, and body is summed up in one verse: Mark 10:46"... blind Bartimaeus, the son of Timaeus, sat by the highway side begging." Again we see one whose state of blindness places him at the mercy of others. This is another example of a physical state that is a spiritual picture of those who cannot see with the eyes of the Spirit. The best one can get is beggarly or meager when they are spiritually blind.

Bartimaeus was positioned "by the highway" or out of the way of life. Isaiah Chapter 35 describes Christ as a Highway and a Way and declares that a wayfaring man, though a fool, cannot err therein. The secret is abiding in the Way once He is known! In spiritual terms, Bartimaeus' physical position was equivalent to being outside the Kingdom of God. Lastly, he was begging. His soul had to be sustained by the generosity of others which may or may not have been consistent or for his good. What his life depended upon was much like the beggarly means and principles of the religious system today.

The glorious day arrived for Bartimaeus' deliverance! Jesus Christ, promised of God to be raised up to sit on David's throne forever, was passing by. It was Bartimaeus' day! Change was imminent! The Son of David was in earshot of him. It was his time! So shall it be for all who seek Christ. Despite the multitude, the Master heard his cry and called Bartimaeus unto Himself. Bartimaeus' action demonstrates restoration of his faith in his spirit, soul and body. Mark 10:50 states, "And he, casting away his garment, rose, and came to Jesus."

His old nature was symbolically cast away. Like Elisha at Elijah's ascension, he took off his own garment. Instead of donning a mantle of uncleanness, Bartimaeus' action depicted one ready to put on righteousness, the Lord Jesus Christ Himself! He *rose*, indicating a resurrection from an old way of life. Finally, he *came to Jesus* in the way. After Jesus declared his faith had made him whole and permitted him to go his own way, immediately he received his sight, and followed Jesus in the way. So Elisha-like!

*Do not neglect your gift, which was given you through prophecy when the body of elders laid their hands on you.*
*1 Timothy 4:14, NIV*

# CHAPTER 14

SAMARIA BESIEGED

As a reminder, Samaria is the home of Elisha, and it means *watch mountain*. How on earth did a watch mountain come under siege? The answer is quite apparent. It is besieged by Ben-hadad which means *son of a false God*! Closely notice and one will detect the similarities of the problem that is going on this very day. There was a great famine in the land. What was normally insignificant now had a high value. For example, the Bible says an ass's head sold for 80 pieces of silver and the fourth part of cab of dove's dung for five pieces of silver (2 Kings 6:25). We will investigate these items later.

The king of Israel was unable to provide relief for the people and when asked for help, sarcastically acknowledged there was nothing in the barn or winepress. There was nothing with which to make bread or wine. "Mission Control" or rather, Heaven, we have a dire problem! Bread and wine speak to the Redemptive Work of Jesus Christ our Lord. No bread or wine! Spiritually, both are compulsory if there is to be effective ministry. No Christ, no ministry! Bread and wine must be served every time the Gospel is preached and while glorious fellowship ensues among brethren. That is the true Communion!

Our barns and winepresses should be overflowing with revelation knowledge of His Broken Body and shed Blood. But, there is no bread or wine in this account with the Samaritans as in several ministries in the earth today. Things are most dismal without what the bread and wine speak of spiritually. Instead, there is ass's head which represents the carnal mind or mind of the wild man, Adam the fallen. Oh, the high price being paid in places for a carnal *CD* or book.

Be keenly aware the real price is always in *silver* which speaks not only to redemption but the trade-off thereof. If one cannot afford the "master prophet's" smoky words, they must settle for the fourth of a cab of dove's dung. What could that possibly be? Some ministers often go to sources other than the Holy Spirit to get a message. It is usually something they perceive to be a move of the Spirit symbolized by a dove, but it is not. Hence it is dove's dung! Notice it is always <u>part</u> (fourth of a cab) and never the complete foursquare or sure Word of Prophecy that glorifies God. Just to be sure one knows, *a cab* is a Hebrew word for a dry measure, and the root meaning of it is to curse.

The situation was so dreadful, two women were in agreement to devour their own sons. One was eaten and other was hid. With a renewed mind, think about the long term spiritual deficit. Without a son, who will bring forth seed? Of course, the king blamed Elisha for the consequences of judgment and sought to kill him. A God-sent prophet never worries about such a threat, and Elisha sat in his house with the elders. Of course, he abides in the Spirit and God is warning him. Elisha saw the king's weak plan unfolding before he ever dispatched his messenger. Consequently, the plan was fully exposed to Elisha who knew the whole scheme in advance. Referring to the king as a murder, Elisha warned the elders to shut the door behind the messenger. The rationale of the king was expressed from his pitiable carnal mind: "Behold, this evil *is* of the LORD; what, do I wait for the LORD any longer?"

Look deeper and one finds that all the situations Elisha was faced with involved some form of death. Ever wonder why? Ponder the meaning of resurrection. Resurrection ministry overcomes death! Jesus called Lazarus' death sleep. The Resurrection is able to bring life to any situation at God's pleasure. Why would Resurrection Life be concerned about death over which It has total victory? Jesus is the Resurrection and the Life. Hopefully, we are grasping the magnitude of the Power that is found only in Him.

Take special note that Elisha spoke what God said about the situation. He did not preach the problem. Some ministers are notorious for preaching the problem. Think how distressing it would be if one went to a doctor considered a specialist, and when describing his symptoms, that doctor simply parroted, "You know, you have headaches, fever, and diarrhea?" One does not want his symptoms rehearsed back by someone, but rather the remedy from one who has the answer. People are seeking a solution that brings healing and wholeness. We have the Healing Solution in Christ the Lord! Preach Him!

To the king's pathetic comment, Elisha replied, "Hear the word of the LORD: thus says the LORD, Tomorrow about this time a measure of fine meal shall be sold for a shekel, and two measures of barley for a shekel, at the gate of Samaria (2 Kings 7:1)." As a nudging reminder, full faith must be in operation if one expects to see the fulfillment of God's promises. Many shall see in this day that people who have nothing religious to filter God's promises through will walk into His unlimited blessings.

Our spiritual example for this declaration is found in the four lepers (sinners) at the gate who woke up to the fact that they should do something instead of just waiting to die. They were not singing "Bye and Bye." From their view and the view of many today, there appears to be an equal chance of survival with the enemy as with the "church folk" who kicked them out. People are confused and find more solace in the world than in the Church. It is true for too many and quite grievous.

The lepers' action speaks to their faith. They rose up and went to the Syrian camp, and there was no man there. Rise up! Do something that makes your faith a counterpart to the Resurrection! They found no man of the Syrians was left. To see no man is a powerful perception! In this victory, the best thing is to see no man! Only the bounty of a supernaturally defeated foe remained. 2 Kings 7:6 says the Lord made the Syrians hear a noise of chariots and a noise of horses. Oh, that sound from heaven! In other words, they heard the sound of the Spiritual Power of God's host ever working on behalf of Elisha and Spirit-filled ministers today.

The enemy thought the king of Israel hired help from the kings of the Hittites and the Egyptians. What is that saying to us in relation to the global situation today in which the Church is just as fearful in places as everyone else? The Hittites were people whose name means *terror*. Terrorists? The very term strikes fear in the hearts of many. Egypt speaks to bondage to the world system. The church is knee-deep in the bondage of the world in too many places today. We are kings and priests not politicians! Trust God and when we stay in our ranks under His authority, the world will submit to Him. Remember, the kingdoms of this world have become the kingdoms of our Lord and His Christ! It is already true in the Spirit, and shall be manifested in the earth by the Spirit.

The Syrians experienced such fear by the Spirit of God, they left their tents, horses, asses, and the camp as it was. Take note that the people in Samaria are still "besieged and fearful" but now without reason. Wake up, Church! The enemy has been defeated by Christ, and their camp is ready for believers to retrieve their stuff. While some are still waiting, others are being laden down with goods as they go from tent to tent.

Suddenly, the lepers realized it was a day of "good tidings." That is so exciting! When a thing is of God it has to be shared! They are experiencing the effect of the Cross. They have to run and tell it! As in the New Testament, run, Mary run! Tell the others He is risen indeed! Run, Peter run, take a look for yourself and see! Run John, your record is really true! There is a Gospel to be preached, so these lepers went and told the porters who informed the king's household.

The king's response to the "good news" was much like some leaders' responses today. Instead of believing and declaring the news, they glorify a defeated enemy. The king thought it was a trap to draw them into the Syrian camp. Regrettably, today there are some who have the nerve to "testify" of how they are battling that "old devil." Why? One of the king's servants was wise enough to employ what speaks to grace. He suggested taking "five" of their remaining horses to go the enemy's camp. God is most merciful! They went all the way to Jordan and found garments and vessels of the Syrians scattered the whole way.

The king finally believed the true report, and the people went out and took the spoils of the Syrians. May God open the eyes of leaders everywhere! May

He allow them to receive the Good News without reservation! In Christ there is no "trap" waiting. Rather, see what happens when we believe the Gospel or Good News? Just like the true prophet said, a measure of fine flour was sold for a shekel, and two measures of barley for a shekel, according to the word of the LORD. Unfortunately, there was one who vehemently refused to receive the word of the prophet and was trampled to death and never partook of the blessing. Be warned in love.

*The prophets prophesy lies, the priests rule
by their own authority, and my people love it
this way. But what will you do in the end?
Jeremiah 5:31, NIV*

# CHAPTER 15

## PROPHETIC MINISTRY BRINGS RESTORATION

There are many other truths that may be gleaned from the ministry of Elisha. One more will be presented by this author before looking briefly at his final miracle. Second Kings 8 tells of Elisha warning the woman whose son he restored to life of a coming famine. She was instructed to go away with her family and stay wherever she could because the famine was to last for seven years. This situation and its duration speaks of a complete emptiness that blazes the way for spiritual perfection that is in progress in the lives of many today. The woman was obedient, and she and her family stayed in the land of the Philistines seven years. Remember, she was a prominent woman.

The Philistines were a perpetual enemy to Israel. The glaring illustration before us is that in a time of famine, what symbolizes the Church was abiding in the land of the enemy. Judgment is ongoing but through it all, the godly ones are being preserved. When seven years ended, the woman returned and went to the king seeking to have her house and land restored. Gehazi, Elisha's servant was rehearsing all the great things Elisha had done to the king, and as he was speaking particularly about the restoring of the woman's son, she showed up to make her request to the king. With astonishment, Gehazi proclaimed, this is the woman and her son! She confirmed her miracle to the king.

Let us not miss any of this great work of restoration. Every detail is fully charged with revelation knowledge. Hopefully, the reader remembers that Gehazi was sent away leprous after receiving reward from Hamaan, but is now testifying before the king of Elisha's powerful miracles. He was proclaiming the heavenly record. The witness of that record was the woman and her son, conveying the restored Church. God's ways are past finding out indeed! To experience the ways of the Spirit is like being suspended in the moment of intensity of a blast at the point where its energy is transmitted outward except it never abates. This is why no flesh can abide His Presence. God is great!

The king appointed a certain officer, again a type of the Spirit, to give back everything that belonged to the woman including all the produce, crops, and revenue from her land from the day she left the country until now. It is worth reading carefully again. All the fruits of her field since the day she left the land (seven years) were restored! Be not dismayed. Questions swirl in our finite minds at such glorious truth. One might wonder, how was the fruit or produce of seven years preserved? This speaks to us of the perfection of spiritual fruit which does not decay! The greater amazement is how there was fruit in the first place in a famine? Eternal Spirit is in operation here. There is no such thing as death in any form able to exalt itself against the knowledge of Christ. Nothing is lost to the Church of the Living God. A totally different Economy is in force now. Restoration is here!

*Blessed is the one who reads aloud the words of this prophecy, and blessed are those who hear it and take to heart what is written in it, because the time is near.*
*Revelation 1:3, NIV*

# CHAPTER 16

A MIRACLE PERFORMED
EVEN IN DEATH!

Let us take only a snapshot of Elisha's last miracle. He became sick. The king of Israel, Joash at the time, wept over him but said something forceful. He said, "O my father, my father, the chariot of Israel, and the horsemen thereof." Sound familiar? The Power and Presence of God were still with Elisha as the day he took up Elijah's mantle. Not one smidgen of it had diminished. This was God's faithful servant. Even in sickness, his ministry continued as he instructed the king. With his hands upon the king's, toward the east or a New Day, together they released the arrow of the Lord's deliverance and deliverance from Syria.

Elisha died and was buried. At the beginning of the year, Moabites, again speaking to multiplied flesh, invaded the land and were burying a man. Be mindful that if not completely destroyed, flesh simply regroups and shows back up when it perceives an opportunity to find place unhindered. When the Moabites saw a band of men, in haste they cast the dead man into the sepulchre of Elisha. When the man was let down and touched the bones of Elisha, he revived and stood up on his feet.

This indicates in the strongest way that physical death is not the end for us. The Son of man was lifted up so that whosoever believes in Him should not perish, but have eternal life (John 3:15). "And this is the record, that God has given to us eternal life, and this life is in his Son (1 John 5:11)." How empowering to read 1 John 5:20 which solemnly and emphatically says, "We know also that the Son of God has come and has given us understanding, so that we may know him who is true. And we are in him who is true by being in his Son Jesus Christ. He is the true God and eternal life." Lastly, John 17:3 is the sum: "And this is life eternal, that they might know thee the only true God, and Jesus Christ, whom thou hast sent."

Again, this whole glorious matter has been about Resurrection Life Power. The defeat of the last enemy, Death, has been prominently exhibited. Jesus Christ, the Resurrection and the Life has all power given unto Him. With the same desire expressed by the Apostle Paul, if only we could truly know Him and the Power of His Resurrection! This last miracle of Elisha with its undiminished, eternal Potency even in physical death assures us of Eternal Life. This, precious saints, is the splendor of the gift of God (Roman 6:23). O grave, where is thy victory?

The Apostle Paul further gives us a glimpse into the mindset of a true servant of God leading up to his or her transition. He told the Philippians (1:23) that he was in a strait and torn between two. He had a desire to depart and be with Christ, which he considered by far the better. The alternative was to remain in the body as he phrased it, which was more necessary for them. Like Paul, we are alive to help others progress in the journey. Jesus promised the Helper would come. The Helper lives in and works through us. To go on living meant fruitful labor for Paul, and that is what it should mean for us all.

As we leave this dynamic Old Covenant example represented by the life and ministry of Elisha, we will go to the New Covenant and layer the resurrections Jesus performed in His earthly ministry. As we have laid the magnificent Pattern of Christ over Elisha, we will now have the opportunity to see how profoundly Elisha's ministry foreshadowed the Lord's. Prayerfully, the remaining chapters will provide further clarity as we explore four eye-opening scenarios including: the significance of the conditions for a death-denying miracle; Jesus' location at the time of the miracles; their three-fold meaning; and the key witnesses present. Upon completion of these areas we shall review the way of the Spirit from an Old Testament perch.

*At this I fell at his feet to worship him. But he said to me, "Don't do that! I am a fellow servant with you and with your brothers and sisters who hold to the testimony of Jesus. Worship God! For it is the Spirit of prophecy who bears testimony to Jesus."*
*Revelation 19:10, NIV*

# CHAPTER 17

꩜

## *JESUS IN ACTION*
## *PART 1*
### *(CONDITIONS FOR A DEATH-DENYING MIRACLE)*

As we seek to apprehend the eternal greatness of Resurrection Power, we shall examine the miracles where Jesus raised the dead, each providing the privilege of a unique aspect of His Power. Expect to be blessed but bear in mind that when done, we will have only tapped meagerly into His unsearchable riches. This statement reflects on our finite abilities rather than the infinite Wisdom of God.

Every Word uttered and every Act committed by our Lord Jesus Christ contained astonishing truth and power for the life of the believer. Such wonderment is not intended to simply awe us as today's watered-down term suggests, but rather to convince us to exchange our minds for His. The Greek word, *existemi*, used to describe the astonishing acts of Christ literally means *to be put out of one's mind*. Our English word *ecstasy* is derived from its noun form. Let us now enter into the Divine as we direct our gaze on what Jesus has done for us and as us. Study the inserted Scriptures below before proceeding.

Scripture Reading Mark 5: 21-24, 35-43

5:21 And when Jesus was passed over again by ship unto the other side, much people gathered unto him: and he was nigh unto the sea.

5:22 And, behold, there cometh one of the rulers of the synagogue, Jairus by name; and when he saw him, he fell at his feet,

5:23 And besought him greatly, saying, My little daughter lieth at the point of death: [I pray thee], come and lay thy hands on her, that she may be healed; and she shall live.

5:24 And [Jesus] went with him; and much people followed him, and thronged him.

5:35 While he yet spake, there came from the ruler of the synagogue's [house certain] which said, Thy daughter is dead: why troublest thou the Master any further?

5:36 As soon as Jesus heard the word that was spoken, he saith unto the ruler of the synagogue, Be not afraid, only believe.

5:37 And he suffered no man to follow him, save Peter, and James, and John the brother of James.

5:38 And he cometh to the house of the ruler of the synagogue, and seeth the tumult, and them that wept and wailed greatly.

5:39 And when he was come in, he saith unto them, Why make ye this ado, and weep? the damsel is not dead, but sleepeth.

5:40 And they laughed him to scorn. But when he had put them all out, he taketh the father and the mother of the damsel, and them that were with him, and entereth in where the damsel was lying.

5:41 And he took the damsel by the hand, and said unto her, Talitha cumi; which is, being interpreted, Damsel, I say unto thee, arise.

5:42 And straightway the damsel arose, and walked; for she was [of the age] of twelve years. And they were astonished with a great astonishment.

5:43 And he charged them straitly that no man should know it; and commanded that something should be given her to eat.

It is necessary to our understanding to see first of all the conditions that had to be met in order for Jesus to raise Jairus' daughter. What exactly were the circumstances affecting the situation. First, Jairus approached Jesus for help in the proper manner. Before anything else, he worshipped the Lord and then made his faith-filled request known. The level of his faith is easily gauged in his certainty of her recovery from the point of death simply by Jesus coming and laying His Hands on her. Once Jesus determined to go with Jairus, her healing was unstoppable even by death. The news of her death did not dissuade Jesus in the least. In the fact and face of death, the Lord said, *"Be not afraid, only believe."*

Again, at this point we are only dealing with the conditions being met in order to receive this miracle. Next, Jesus took only three of His disciples with Him to Jairus' house. Despite the huge crowd just "pumped up" by the healing of the woman with the issue of blood, only three of His disciples were taken with Him. Oh, the difference in witnessing His Power and partaking of It. When Jesus arrived on the scene where death flaunted its temporary victory and mourners writhed under its devastating sting, He authoritatively questioned their behavior in the wake of what was simply "sleep" to Him. In their desperation, doubt and unbelief, death was reigning unhindered. However, the Author of Life entered and pronounced to all that death is only a humbled state of sleep in His Presence.

Their unbelief was punctuated by their ridicule of Jesus. As long as the circumstance is given a superior place to Jesus, there is no place for a miracle to operate. That crowd had to be put out! Hallelujah! The conditions of a miracle must be exact. The Master is the Remedy, and He knows what must be present to execute a miracle. Only Jairus and his wife were allowed to stay. Observe the remnant with Jesus through the eyes of the Spirit. Three disciples plus the child's parents! An exact total of five which is God's number for His wondrous grace. Jesus and grace! Miracles are never earned. Miracles are the result of grace! Grace and truth came by Jesus Christ! Although Jairus was a ruler in the synagogue, his status meant nothing in getting a miracle from God. While his status counted for nothing, his faith in God counted for everything and ushered grace and Resurrection Life Power into his situation. With only Jesus and grace present, He lifted the child by the hand and commanded her to arise. Glory to the Lamb of God!

In the next miracle, we shall attentively review the raising of the son of the widow of Nain from the dead. In the following verses from Luke we again focus only on the conditions that were met for the execution of this powerful miracle:

> 7:11 And it came to pass the day after, that he went into a city called Nain; and many of his disciples went with him, and much people.

7:12 Now when he came nigh to the gate of the city, behold, there was a dead man carried out, the only son of his mother, and she was a widow: and much people of the city was with her.

7:13 And when the Lord saw her, he had compassion on her, and said unto her, Weep not.

7:14 And he came and touched the bier: and they that bare [him] stood still. And he said, Young man, I say unto thee, Arise.

7:15 And he that was dead sat up, and began to speak. And he delivered him to his mother.

7:16 And there came a fear on all: and they glorified God, saying, That a great prophet is risen up among us; and, That God hath visited his people.

7:17 And this rumour of him went forth throughout all Judaea, and throughout all the region round about.

When examining the conditions surrounding this miracle, the compassion of the Lord is the centerpiece. Jesus pitied the widow. In the Book of James it reads, "...the LORD is very pitiful and of tender mercy." James 5:11. The word used to express *pitiful* in this verse is the extreme of the word *compassion* from Luke's Gospel above. James is conveying that the Lord or *Kurios* which means the *Owner*, is extremely compassionate and of tender mercy. Throughout the New Covenant all the way to the Cross, compassion is a distinctive feature of the Lord Jesus.

James continues to shed light on the conditions for this great miracle of mastering death. We shall see it momentarily. Throughout Scripture it is readily noted that God loves the widows and the orphans. In Exodus 22:22-23 it states, "Ye shall not afflict any widow, or fatherless child. If thou afflict them in any wise, and they cry at all unto Me, I will surely hear their cry;" James 1:27 reads, "Pure religion and undefiled before God and the Father is this, to <u>visit</u> (underline added for emphasis) the fatherless and the widows in their affliction, and to keep himself unspotted from the world." Did you notice the people responded to the miracle of raising the widows son by saying "...God hath visited his people?" Jesus visited the fatherless and the widow in their affliction indeed!

Pure religion and undefiled along with God's compassion create another ripe atmosphere for complete victory over death. Jesus knew no sin but became sin for us. As an undefiled and obedient Son of God, He moved mightily in power and demonstration of the Spirit no matter what event challenged Him. A touch from the Master's undefiled Hand rendered death totally ineffective.

So far we have seen Jesus and grace as well as compassion without defilement create conditions of marvel as the miraculous Power of God raised the dead. Death found no place for struggle and could by no means wrest itself from the Grip of Resurrection Life. This scene encapsulates heaven in miniature, but the miracle about to be performed by Jesus had heaven's full weight of glory behind it.

As the conditions for the miracles intensify with the raising of Lazarus after being dead four days, let us read thoroughly this scene in depth surrounding this extraordinary miracle. To get the full impact of this lesson, one must read the entirety of John 1:1-43.

The sisters of Lazarus, Mary and Martha, represent types of ministries that will contribute to the conditions of this death-denying miracle. Lazarus was sick, and both of his sisters (ministries) sent word to Jesus. The message emphasized "he whom thou lovest is sick." The word used for *sick* carries a meaning of a sickness where one is in serious decline and death is imminent. That is the precise condition of man apart from Christ. Because of the Fall, every man is spiritually dead, and despite physical life, the state of death persists apart from God. It is profound that the Lord is reminded of His love for Lazarus by his sisters. "For God so loved the world that He gave His only begotten Son that whosoever believeth in Him should not perish but have eternal life" (John 3:16).

Jesus, the Resurrection and the Life, received the news of Lazarus' condition. Despite His great love for Lazarus, He could not proceed without Father's permission. Father had a season for His Son to be glorified. In His glory, Jesus would undo the work of the adversary in the Fall. As Messiah, He had a precise Plan to follow. All the way to the Cross, His actions in all things were manifesting Father's Thoughts. Eternal Power was being demonstrated in every parable, healing, teaching, and movement, fulfilling all that the Law and prophets spoke of. Again unmoved by the threat of death, He moved fearlessly at Father's command.

"Then when Jesus came, he found that he had lain in the grave four days already (John 11:17)."

According to the Companion Bible margin note for this verse, in that day, the rabbis taught that the spirit of a dead person wandered about for three days seeking readmission into the body but abandoned it on the fourth day because corruption had set in. The above passage describes precisely the state of man in Adam or the fallen state at the time of Jesus' earthly ministry. "But beloved, be not ignorant of this one thing, one day is with the Lord as a thousand years, and a thousand years as one day" (2 Peter 3:8).

From Adam to Christ is 4,000 years or *four days*. Ponder the corruption of mankind after centuries of spiritual death. Everything Jesus did revealed an aspect of Himself as the Lord of heaven. He abode two more days after getting the news of Lazarus because Father's Word (Jesus) was being fulfilled. There had to be no doubt of corruption if Incorruption was to be manifested. The Cross was fast approaching and Jesus was about to perform a miracle that spoke to the very miracle of salvation.

Let us focus again on the two types of ministry that directly affect the conditions of this miracle. Martha, or cumbered ministry, goes to meet Jesus. While she begins to proclaim truths concerning Him, her knowledge of Him is not guided by understanding. That happens quite often today and, it means simply a lack of revelation of the true Life, Ministry, and Gospel of Jesus Christ our Lord. For example, today in many ministries, there are a lot of truths rehearsed about and unto the Lord; however, there is no spiritual understanding of what those truths mean. Martha even demonstrates her faith. The fact of the matter is that real faith toward God is executed from a position of rest in Him. It proceeds from peace instead of anxiety.

Mary, on the contrary, representing the ministry that actually touched the Lord, remained still in the house. Mary, or ministry that touches the Lord, did not move until she received word that He called her. What a profound revelation if ministry everywhere responded only when called upon by the Lord. Not only did she move at His call, but she moved quickly. By moving quickly at the call of God, we deny the adversary of any chance of talking us out of our purpose. Notice that Jesus remained in the place where Martha met Him.

There is no mention of anyone following Martha to Jesus. However, the people followed Mary. It is time for every ministry to acknowledge whether or not it is taking people to Jesus on His terms. There is a huge difference in teaching Adam, the fallen man, to be successful in the things of this world, and leading the Jews (spiritual Israel) to our Lord.

When Mary approached Jesus, the first thing she did was worship Him. What a contrast to Martha. Prayerfully, we can see the power of approaching God in the correct manner. Mary's actions are akin to Jairus' when he sought Jesus' help on behalf of his daughter. It is fine to make our requests known but only after we have approached Him properly in worship. Once Mary worshipped Jesus, then she made her request known, which, if observed carefully in reading John 11, was verbatim to Martha's statement. It requires ministry full of faith that praises and worships the Lord to move Him into the situation of need. The condition for the miracle is coming into clear view now.

When Jesus saw Mary and the Jews weeping, He groaned in the spirit and was troubled. Weeping speaks to true repentance. Repentance tells God that He is right and we are wrong. He is our only Answer! Repentance proceeds from a pure heart. Heaven then takes notice. Ministry as represented by Mary touched Jesus to the point of moving Him from that place directly to Lazarus' grave. Apart from Christ, man's body of earth is a grave, because it contains a dead man. True ministry brings resurrection life to the situation.

Did you notice that Jesus wept also? In the other miracles above He did not weep. Yet here He is found completely identifying with the state of man. This death affected his friends. We are His friends! Again, we find the incomprehensible compassion that only a loving Creator can express. God's Love was being manifested in their midst. His Love is evident in His presence. Notice how much of the weight of the condition for the miracle is now upon ministry or God's people.

As a result of a ministry that took the people to Jesus and brought Jesus into the situation as exemplified in Mary's actions, the faith of the people increased. They began to rehearse other miraculous works such as the opening of blind eyes. Their faith reached a level that made them ask whether Jesus could in fact have kept Lazarus from dying. Great faith! Once our spiritual sight is open, faith is increased and it becomes much easier to expect no less than His Resurrection Power. This worship-filled atmosphere with fully submitted and expectant believers caused a condition where faith was ready to shake hands in reverent unity with God's Power. A foretaste of Immortality swallowing up mortality is at hand. Corruption heaves helplessly as it is forced to fully yield to Incorruption. All the Master has to do in this condition is simply say, "Lazarus, Come forth!"

*I have also spoken by the prophets, and I have mul-
tiplied visions, and used similitudes, by the ministry
of the prophets.*
*Hosea 12:10, KJV*

# Chapter 18

## Jesus in Action
## Part 2
### (A Three-Fold Perspective of Resurrection)

Now that we have learned the conditions for a death-denying miracle, we will continue to layer those instances of truth with a three-fold dimension of Resurrection. Man is a triune being. We are spirit; we have a soul; and we live in a body. Always from the perspective of the Divine, there are only two men in the earth. Regardless of race, color or creed, every human being is either in one or the other of these two, Adam or Christ. Adam, the first man, is of the earth, and he is earthy. The second, the Lord Jesus Christ is the Lord from heaven *(1 Corinthians 15:47)*.

According to *Romans 6:23* we have clearly seen that Adam got paid, and we all experienced the effect of the wages for his sin (spiritual death). Through Christ we have been redeemed or bought out of that condition of spiritual death and restored to Father's Presence and favor. This wondrous Plan of Redemption is being viewed through the multiple layers of Divine Accomplishment found in the three miraculous instances where Jesus raised the dead.

There are literally volumes of riches concerning our restoration contained in each instance. There are numerous unveilings in these three miracles which are easily applied to us as triune beings if seen through the Spirit. In the stages of spiritual maturity, we go from being a child to a young man then on to a full grown man. Whether our natural gender is male or female, it is all Christ at this point and none of those carnal attributes matter at all.

Let us now refresh the account of the raising of Jairus' daughter from Mark 5:35-43. In this miracle Jesus raised a child from the dead. She was twelve years old or Jesus' exact age when He set out to be about His Father's business. When we mean business with God, we will find that he has already taken care of business. As previously developed, Jesus and "grace" (as represented by the five people present at her resurrection) were the Catalyst for this miracle. Our attention is invited again to Mark 5:41. The main purpose at this point is to capture the spiritual level being dealt with in each miracle. "And he took the damsel by the hand, and said unto her, Talitha cumi; which is, being interpreted, Damsel, I say unto thee, arise."

The Lord is showing mankind what He did in His Cross to save us in this tiny verse of Scripture. He took this little girl by the hand. This is the only miracle of the three where Jesus physically touched the body of the dead. It is in what He said that unleashes the power enlaced in this passage. "Talitha cumi." Cumi is an Aramaic variation of *qum*. Here is the only place this Aramaic word is found in the New Testament. Is that not a wonder? Although cumi means *arise*, *qum*, of which it is a variation, means *lifted up*. The following verses from John Chapter Three will help us see more clearly.

> John 3:14 And as Moses lifted up the serpent in the wilderness, even so must the Son of man be lifted up:
>
> 3:15 That whosoever believeth in him should not perish, but have eternal life.
>
> 3:16 For God so loved the world, that he gave his only begotten Son, that whosoever believeth in him should not perish, but have everlasting life.
>
> 3:17 For God sent not his Son into the world to condemn the world; but that the world through him might be saved.

Let us go back to the Old Testament and see what necessitated Moses lifting up a serpent in the wilderness. The incident is found in Numbers 21:4-9, and we will revisit it in a subsequent chapter. However, it needs to be especially highlighted here. Amazingly, it was the soul of the People that was much grieved and impatient because of the way. The soul, which enthrones the human mind, will, and emotions, is the initial entry through which our change comes. We must decide to receive Jesus.

Once we accept Jesus Christ as our Lord and Savior, we begin our child-like step on a pilgrimage that will take us fully into the Prize of the high calling found only in Him. Our spirits are regenerated or made alive when we say yes to Jesus and receive Him as Savior and Lord. The Seed that Christ is becomes planted within us, and all that is needed to bring us to full maturity as a son of God is packed into us even when we are spiritual children. Glory to God!

It is hoped the reader recognized that of the three miracles of resurrection, this female child is the first. She is a distinct picture of a soul yielding to the Power of God. David referred to his soul as the feminine gender when he said, "My soul shall make her boast in the Lord" (Psalm 34:2). Again, this is but the first step of a Spirit-guided journey unto full maturity as a son of God.

Returning to the wilderness experience of the children of Israel, we find the discouragement of the people caused them to speak against God and Moses and emphasize how their *souls* loathed God's provision. Every believer needs to be taught early how the only thing that awaits a fleshy preference is a serpent encounter. The serpent was cursed to eat dust which flesh was made from. God is not a cruel God. He is a Perfect, Loving Father. His only provision for flesh or dust is for the serpent to eat it. The people did not want His spiritual provision (Manna) which pictured Christ and Life, so the only alternative was flesh and its sinful wages or death.

Our Heavenly Father is always moved by and lovingly responds to the truly repentant heart; therefore at their repentance and cry for Him to take away the fiery serpents, through Moses' prayer, God sent His remedy to take away the death from among them. The instructions were for Moses to make a fiery serpent of brass and set it upon a pole. When *everyone* that was bitten looked upon it, he lived. These events were types and shadows for our learning. The truth of the matter is that we were born under this curse of death from the serpent's bite.

Jesus Christ fulfilled that type as the serpent on a pole when He was lifted up on Calvary and fully identified with our sin nature. John 3:14 declares, "And as Moses lifted up the serpent in the wilderness, even so must the Son of man be lifted up." He was obedient unto death, even the death of the Cross. Realizing His Purpose as Savior of the world meant He must be lifted up onto the Cross, He could proclaim, *Talitha cumi*! Thank you, Jesus!

See why the Gospel must be a constant presentation and demonstration held up so mankind can live. One should ask whether his or her preaching is bringing Life to those who look on what is "lifted up?" Money and other temporal things constantly held before the people will not bring Life for a look as the Gospel does. Hold up the Serpent of Brass or the Redemptive Work of the Cross so all may see the judgment of this world and live. Please do not allow the Power of the Gospel to become like Nehushtan *(2 Kings 18:4)*, an idol with no meaning and a mere piece of brass. The true meaning of the Serpent of Brass on a pole is the very Cross of Christ in type and is therefore our very Life.

Jesus said again in John 8: 28, "... When ye have lifted up the Son of man, then shall ye know that I am [he], and [that] I do nothing of myself; but as my Father hath taught me, I speak these things." Again in John 12: 32 "And I, if I be lifted up from the earth, will draw all men unto Me." The essence of this verse is seen when Jesus lifted Jairus' little daughter by the hand. Hallelujah!

We shall now look into the next spiritual level or the raising of the *young man*, the only son of the widow of Nain. This level of maturity means much planting and watering are ongoing and increase, which can only come from God, is break-ing forth. However, there is much more development required for a full grown son. This is a level of learning and experiencing the things of God. At this level the believer is no longer a child but is still unable to see through the eyes of perfection. He is unable to see the deep things of God. For instance, in the Book of Ruth, Boaz (Our Kinsman Redeemer) had to protect Ruth (the Church) from the *young men* by charging them not to touch or molest or trouble her (Ruth 2:9). Anything less than the full Thought and Will of God has the potential to vex rather than help. Although the *young man* is in an advancing state, he is yet well shy of complete maturation in the Spirit.

To gain further insight into this stage of the young man, one may read Genesis 22:19 which concerns the offering of Isaac. Abraham took two young men with him. They were allowed to go on the journey with Abraham but could only go so far. On the third day when Abraham saw the place afar off, he told the young men to stay with the ass while he and the lad, Isaac, continued to the place to worship. What is so wonderful about Abraham's statement is that he told the young men he and Isaac would come again to them. What assurance of faith was in operation! It most certainly does not sound like a normal man about to offer his only son; therefore, God was with him! God commanded Abraham to offer Isaac whom God called Abraham's *only son*. As one recalls, Isaac did have a brother after the flesh and all things are entirely spiritual now.

What was about to take place at Mount Moriah was a spiritual type of the offering of Jesus or God's *only Begotten Son*. Abraham would carry out the ultimate selfless task of not withholding his only son from God. In other words, the ultimate act of worship or worship in spirit and in truth was about to take place.

The *young men* accompanying Abraham further represent a spiritual level where such Divine discipline is still being inwrought in their hearts by the Power of God. They would not have been able to apprehend the Power of this type of worship even though it would have happened right in front of their eyes. This type of worship cannot be emulated or feigned. This type of worship is an expression of the fullness of Whom It is dwelling inside the individual giving the offering.

After God provided Himself a ram just as Emmanuel (God with us) provided Himself a Sacrifice for our sin, Abraham returned to the *young men* in possession of God's blessing and Isaac, his son. God's blessing goes so much farther than personal, temporary goodies. God's blessing is eternal and is designed to impact the nations of the earth. *Young men* become stretched to "think outside the box" of self until self, like Abraham, is gone and all that matters is Father's Plan and Purpose in Christ Jesus His Son. One should ask himself if the blessing he longs for will affect the entire world?

Now may we go to the raising of the young man in Luke's Gospel and see what

Jesus showed us concerning this spiritual level of development. Focus on Luke 7:11-17 from the previous chapter. Jesus touched the *bier* and not the body as He did with Jairus's daughter. Noah Webster's 1828 *American Dictionary of the English Language* defines a *bier* as a carriage or frame for conveying dead human bodies to the grave. Jesus touched the *frame* instead of the young man's corpse. Psalm 103:13-14 states, "Like as father pitieth his children, so the Lord pitieth them that fear him. For he knoweth our frame; he remembers that we are dust." (Underline added for emphasis). The Hebrew word for *frame* is *yetser* which figuratively means *purpose.* It also means *imagination, mind and work.* The prophet Isaiah used this same word in Chapter 29 and verse 16 when he wrote, "...shall the work say of him that made it, He made me not? Or shall the thing framed say of him that framed it, He had no understanding?" The New International Version of this same passage reads, "Can the pot say to the potter, "You know nothing?""

At the spiritual stage of development personified by the young man, the believer puts on the Mind of Christ. Paul quoted Isaiah to the church at Corinth when he wrote: "For who hath known the mind of the LORD, that he may instruct Him? But we have the mind of Christ." Notice Paul added, But we have the mind of Christ! When Jesus touches what represents our minds change comes. His touch of Resurrection Life causes us to re-frame and live through the Mind and Thoughts of our Maker.

In the Old Testament, God put His Spirit in Bezaleel to wrought the work of the Tabernacle with *cunning work. Cunning work* is the Hebrew word *chashab and* is akin to *yester. Chashab* also carries the meaning to think, conceive, and imagine. The spiritual house we are is being fitly framed and joined together into the Tabernacle that Christ is along with His Body. Another glorious picture is in Solomon's Temple (1 Kings 6:7). The *young men* are being made ready in the quarry before being brought to the temple as living stones and are then set. In this Spiritual House there is no sound of a hammer or axe or any tool of iron heard while it is in building. The Work is finished! It is all a walk of faith in the Spirit at this point.

Luke 7:14 "Young man, I say unto thee, arise" is now our center of interest. While the Master did not touch the young man's body, He did touch the "frame" that speaks foremost to the mind. One of the Apostle Paul's main concerns for the church at Corinth was that their minds might be corrupted from the simplicity in Christ. There is another gospel, another Jesus, and another spirit vying for our minds (2 Corinthians 11:4). The only escape from the false is to be touched by the True.

This is why Jesus spoke to the young man and said *arise*. The word arise here literally means to *awake from sleep*. It is a different word than *cumi* which was used for Jairus' daughter to arise. Now that we have been *lifted up* to new life as children, as *young men* we have to wake out of sleep. We have to wake up to all that is true of us in the risen Christ! The preaching or teaching or speaking of the Gospel unto the *young men* contains the Power of God unto salvation. Faith comes by hearing and hearing by the Word of God.

It is time to wake out of sleep. Let us see what Paul told the church at Ephesus about waking out of sleep. Remember, Paul is addressing believers!

Ephesians 5: 13-21 reads:

5:13 But all things that are reproved are made manifest by the light: for whatsoever doth make manifest is light.

5:14 Wherefore he saith, Awake thou that sleepest, and arise from the dead, and Christ shall give thee light.

5:15 See then that ye walk circumspectly, not as fools, but as wise,

5:16 Redeeming the time, because the days are evil.

5:17 Wherefore be ye not unwise, but understanding what the will of the Lord [is].

5:18 And be not drunk with wine, wherein is excess; but be filled with the Spirit;

5:19 Speaking to yourselves in psalms and hymns and spiritual songs, singing and making melody in your heart to the Lord;

5:20 Giving thanks always for all things unto God and the Father in the name of our Lord Jesus Christ;

5:21 Submitting yourselves one to another in the fear of God.

*Young men* are being clothed in Light. They are putting on the Lord Jesus Christ! Paul says the same thing in verse fourteen above as Jesus spoke to the corpse of the *young man.* The above verses from Ephesians contain powerful instruction for the *young men.* Romans 13:11-14 also serves as a "wake-up call" for this stage of spiritual growth and development. It reads: "And that, knowing the time, that now [it is] high time to awake out of sleep: for now [is] our salvation nearer than when we believed. The night is far spent, the day is at hand: let us therefore cast off the works of darkness, and let us put on the armour of light. Let us walk honestly, as in the day; not in rioting and drunkenness, not in chambering and wantonness, not in strife and envying. But put ye on the Lord Jesus Christ, and make not provision for the flesh, to [fulfil] the lusts [thereof]." Our salvation is nearer than when we believed or were a little child as Jairus' daughter. Let us go on to perfection!

The full grown man pictured by Lazarus is the final stage of spiritual development we shall endeavor to gain insight into. Let us quickly review only a few verses from John 11. Verses 39-44 read:

11:39 Jesus said, Take ye away the stone. Martha, the sister of him that was dead, saith unto him, Lord, by this time he stinketh: for he hath been [dead] four days.

11:40 Jesus saith unto her, Said I not unto thee, that, if thou wouldest believe, thou shouldest see the glory of God?

11:41 Then they took away the stone [from the place] where the dead was laid. And Jesus lifted up [his] eyes, and said, Father, I thank thee that thou hast heard me.

11:42 And I knew that thou hearest me always: but because of the people which stand by I said [it], that they may believe that thou hast sent me.

11:43 And when he thus had spoken, he cried with a loud voice, Lazarus, come forth.

11:44 And he that was dead came forth, bound hand and foot with grave-clothes: and his face was bound about with a napkin. Jesus saith unto them, Loose him, and let him go.

As seen earlier, corruption has had time to set in with Lazarus. This was not the case with Jairus' little daughter or the young man who was the son of the widow of Nain. This view of the resurrection of the full grown man wherein lies corruption will help us gain further revelation into the Power of His Resurrection. The Apostle Paul's cry even after personally meeting the Resurrected Christ was a yearning to know Him and the Power of His Resurrection. Oh that we may all be blessed with intimate knowledge of all Christ and His Resurrection accomplished in all realms.

The *full grown man* speaks to spiritual maturity. Maturity in the spirit means absolutely no works of the flesh. Zero flesh! Jesus moved out into His earthly ministry only after passing every test of the flesh. Remember, He was driven by the Spirit into the wilderness and He overcame. Praise God for the Ministry of the Holy Ghost. The lusts of the flesh circumvent the walk in the Spirit. We have to pass the tests of the lust of the eyes and of the flesh, and the great granddaddy of them all, the pride of life. Be assured that we must be filled with the Spirit to do so.

The full grown son like Abraham knows at this point it is all Father's will and good pleasure or nothing at all. These tests are passed only in Christ. The sequel of any single-handed, lone ranger, or rogue effort on our part is disaster. Through our God we shall do valiantly! Our lives are hid with Christ in God at this point. Corruption puts on Incorruption, and He is magnificent in His victory. Death, where is thy sting? Death and hell have surrendered fully to Christ in Whom sons are clothed! The grave has lost its victory. All grave clothes have been cast off. Hallelujah! Every crown is cast before Him!

Notice Jesus did not lift the *full grown man* by the hand, neither did he touch the place where he lay. He simply spoke the Language of the Spirit and the Bride and said, *Lazarus, Come forth. Come forth* means literally to *come hither or come out.* John on the Isle of Patmos was *in the Spirit* on the Lord's Day. It was in the Spirit that John wrote the Revelation or Unveiling of Jesus Christ. John immediately informs the blessed reader of the Book of Revelation that he was in the Spirit, yet he is beckoned higher and higher to be shown things concerning Christ and His Bride. Note the following passages where underlines are added for emphasis:

Revelation 17:1-3a

"And there came one of the seven angels which had the seven vials, and talked with me, saying unto me, Come hither; I will shew unto thee the judgment of the great whore that sitteth upon many waters: With whom the kings of the earth have committed fornication, and the inhabitants of the earth have been made drunk with the wine of her fornication. So he carried me away in the spirit..."

Revelation 18:4

"And I heard another voice from heaven, saying, Come out of her, my people, that ye be not partakers of her sins, and that ye receive not of her plagues."

Revelation 21:9-10

"And there came unto me one of the seven angels which had the seven vials full of the seven last plagues, and talked with me, saying, Come hither, I will shew thee the bride, the Lamb's wife. And he carried me away in the spirit to a great and high mountain, and shewed me that great city, the holy Jerusalem, descending out of heaven from God."

Beyond corruption are many realms of unveilings of our Lord. In the Spirit we see the judgement of this world; our calling out from Babylon or confusion; as well as the Bride of Christ we are from the above passages. Although it is clear from the Word that the Church or Bride of Christ, the Lamb of God, descends, it is widely taught that she goes up. Apparently, the confusion lies in the fact that such a teacher is not a mature man as represented in the raising of Lazarus. The mature one in the Spirit sees her descending out of heaven from God. The immature one is unaware that we are already seated together with Christ in heavenly places (Ephesians 2:6).

How sobering it is to see that the real walk or life in the Spirit commences at death to self. Only when there is no chance of the old man coming back does the Power and the Glory reveal Himself. Our God is a Consuming Fire, and at His holy Presence, we are loosed and set free. As Shadrach, Meshach and Abednego, only that which binds us is burned off and we see assuredly that whom the Son sets free is free indeed. Yes, the *form (root meaning: to show self, see, perceive or discern)* of the fourth man is the like the Son of God. Christ as Incorruption consumes corruption!

These three men in the Old Testament account of Daniel also mirrored the three stages of spiritual development seen as Jesus raised the dead during His earthly ministry. Returning to their Hebrew names, we see a most powerful reflection. Dear reader, you have a new name in the Lord Jesus Christ, and name connotes nature. It is not the name or nature you received in your spiritual captivity from the "Babylonians" while mired in confusion. Death reigns in confusion, and only the Son of God can deliver us from its grip.

Shadrach's true name was Hananiah *(Daniel 1:6)*, which means *Jah has favored.* Did we not see *grace* or God's unmerited favor accompany Jesus at the raising of Jairus' daughter? How grace responds to child-like faith! Meshach's true name was Mishael *(Daniel 1:6)*, meaning Who is what God is? or who is strength? It is written in Proverbs 20:29 that, "The glory of young men is their strength..." Rejoice *young men* as you put on Christ, God's strength! Finally, Abednego's true name was Azariah *(Daniel 1:6)* which means *Jah has helped.* That is precisely the meaning of Lazarus' name, *God has helped.* Walk on beloved, until you see by the Spirit that you are he whom God has helped!

*Surely the Lord GOD will do nothing, but he re-*
*vealeth his secret unto his servants the prophets.*
*Amos 3:7, KJV*

# CHAPTER 19

*JESUS IN ACTION
PART 3*

*(KEY WITNESSES TO THE THREE RESURRECTIONS BY JESUS)*

At this juncture, we shall look intently at the key witnesses who were present when Jesus raised these three people from the dead. The multifaceted spiritual mysteries encrypted in these miracles are incomprehensible apart from the Wisdom of God. To be mined, our spirits must be one with His. The Holy Spirit inspired the Gospel writers to include certain details all of which would disclose multiple aspects of His Power. The names and descriptions of the key witnesses or people involved in the miracles speak an abundance of revelation to open hearts seeking to know Jesus and the power of His Resurrection.

In the first miracle of the raising of Jairus' twelve year-old daughter, we have established that Jesus and grace, as pictured by the five others, were present. We must constantly recall that Jesus moved in the fullness of the Power of the Holy Spirit. As stated, names mentioned are loaded with meaning that tells us about God and His Christ. For example, Mark 5:22 clearly states the ruler of the synagogue that came to Jesus was called Jairus by name. Why would the Spirit inspire this much detail? Why not just say, "A ruler of the synagogue?" Eyes anointed with cye-salve can see the meaning of Jairus' name carries intimate detail in some way. Jairus' name means *whom God enlightens.* The root of its meaning is *to be or become light or to shine.*

With Jesus moving in the fullness of the Spirit's Power, that same Power had to be present at the raising of this child. Yes, Jesus possessing the Spirit without measure and grace were all present and accounted for at the raising of Jairus' daughter! Her resurrection pictures the new birth of a saint. When we accept Jesus Christ as our Lord and Savior, we also receive a measure of His Holy Spirit. The Holy Spirit has to be present to baptize us into the Body of Christ at the new birth (First Corinthians 12:13). Let us re-read the account of this miracle from Mark 5:21-24, 35-43, if necessary, with our focus now zoomed on the Holy Ghost's Presence as Baptizer into the Lord's Body in the name Jairus.

There is a brilliant Old Testament type of Jairus found in the Book of Judges by the name of Jair. Jair's name has the same root meaning for Jairus. Jair was a judge raised up by God after the atrocious deception of Abimelech who usurped the judgeship by killing his seventy brethren. Let us very briefly review some details of Jair's judgeship to help reveal what the Spirit would have us see concerning Jairus.

*Judges 10:3 And after him* (Tola) *arose Jair, a Gileadite, and judged Israel twenty and two years.* Jair was a judge in whom God's Plan continued and a solid demonstration of the Holy Spirit's power may be seen in him. He portrays the working of the Holy Spirit within the believer to take him into the measure of the full stature of Christ. God bestows His merciful and gracious Essence upon us at the new birth. Are you beginning to tie this example in with the miracle above?

It would be great for every believer to commit to memory the prayer for revelation the Apostle Paul prayed for the church at Ephesus. Part of his prayer petitioned God to give that church a spirit of wisdom and revelation in the knowledge of Him. He added to that request the following: "The eyes of your understanding being <u>enlightened;</u> (underline for emphasis) that ye may know what is the hope of His calling, and what the riches of the glory of His inheritance in the saints, And what is the exceeding greatness of his power to us-ward who believe, according to the working of His mighty power, which He wrought in Christ, when He raised him from the dead, and set Him at His own right hand in the heavenly places, far above principality, and power, and might, and dominion, and every name that is named, not only in this world, but also in that which is to come: and hath put all things under His feet, and gave Him to be head over all things to the church, which is His body, the fullness of Him that filleth all in all." (Ephesians 1:18-23).

At this point the new creature, as pictured by Jairus' daughter is in union with God. The old death nature has been swallowed up in Christ. There is now a new creation with a new name written in glory. Again, none of the fallen nature has any place in this pure realm with Christ. All emphasis is on the new creation after Christ. All the promises are to the new creation alone. Any thoughts and actions associated with the old nature assure regression at this point. There is no going back now. Going back would mean turning from victory in Jesus to ultimate loss and defeat. Forward movement means progressing to the next stages of spiritual maturity until the believer is a full grown son crying, "Abba Father."

Rehearsing briefly, we have established that Jair means to *enlighten, to become light or to shine*. Here is the key! As we become enlightened in our inner man, the Light of Christ is then reflected from within us; therefore, we shine. The Bible teaches us to let our light so shine before men that they may see our good works and glorify our Father which is in heaven! Jesus said we are the light of the world and should be as a city situated on a hill that cannot be hid (Matthew 5:14). We must be lighted with Him and allow Him to shine from within us.

Jair was a Gileadite. Gilead was known for its medicine or balm. You may remember the Ishmeelites that bought Joseph from his brothers were from Gilead. They were on their way to Egypt to trade the balm, spices and myrrh. (Genesis 37:25). Since Joseph is too a type of the Lord Jesus Christ, we are presented with yet another view of His death for us and as us. His goings forth are truly from of old! The balm speaks to healing. He is the God that heals us!

Jairus' daughter went from sickness unto death to becoming made whole. True healing is spiritual. Contact with Jesus makes one completely whole as He said. Calvary must never be understood as a mysterious *Band Aid* approach to the sinful state of man. At Calvary, death was overcome once for all! This Balm heals all manner of disease. The Balm is the Word made Flesh. We have boldness to enter into the holiest by His Blood by a new and living way which He has consecrated for us through the veil, which is His Flesh (Hebrews 10:19-20). A study of balm in Scripture reveals that it is a substance that leaks from a tree that is cracked open from pressure. How compelling in light of Jesus' Sacrifice for us. He said the Holy Spirit would take of His and show it unto us. Spiritual illumination of our Lord is what Jair and Jairus signify!

Notice Jair is named but no lineage is given. From this perspective, he is seen spiritually as one without father or mother. Please hear what the Spirit is saying. Who else do we read of without descent other than Melchizedek, King of righteousness, Priest of the Most High, after Whose Order Christ is? (Hebrews 7:3). The Spirit of our High Priest was on the scene at Jairus' house that wondrous day, and He was indeed ministering out of an Endless Life.

*Judges 10:4-5 And he had thirty sons that rode on thirty ass colts, and they had thirty cities, which are called Havothjair unto this day, which [are] in the land of Gilead. And Jair died, and was buried in Camon.*

While there is no lineage, the Scriptures go on to declare all Jair had. *Thirty sons that rode on thirty ass colts, and they had thirty cities!* The possession detailed here is so ripe with revelation until it is hard to know where to begin. First of all, thirty speaks of maturity according to *Appendix Ten of The Companion Bible.* At the new birth, again, as pictured in the miracle at Jairus' house, all that is needed to take us into maturity is made in a giant Deposit of the Seed of Christ in our spirits. We must keep our eyes on the Forerunner as we are changed into His Image spiritual step by spiritual step. Hallelujah!

Take a refreshing breath to see where maturity lands a believer. First, there is the example of Joseph who is a type of Christ. "And Joseph was thirty years old when he stood or took office before Pharaoh king of Egypt. And Joseph went out from the presence of Pharaoh and went throughout all the land of Egypt." (Genesis 41:46). Secondly, there is David, the great king after God's own heart. "David was thirty years old when he began to reign, and he reigned forty years." (II Samuel 5:4). Next, there is Ezekiel, God's messenger in a time of gross darkness and bondage. "Now it came to pass in the thirtieth year, in the fourth month, in the fifth day of the month, as I was among the captives by the river of Chebar, that the heavens were opened, and I saw visions of God." (Ezekiel 1:1).

Well, we see in Joseph that in maturity one is able to face off with our enemy and walk away unharmed with all power throughout the enemy's jurisdiction. Secondly, David, the greatest king that ever lived began to reign at the age of maturity. Given an everlasting kingdom, even our Lord is referred to as the Son of David. Yet again in Ezekiel, we find heaven opened upon a mature one despite being in captivity. Finally, the greatest Example of maturity is seen Luke 3:23, "And Jesus himself began to be about thirty years of age..." Jesus began to be! This is what it is all about! This is the sum of all that is written and said. Just begin to be! Just be light! Just let your Light shine before men! It is not a little light but a great Light!

Jair's thirty sons speak to a mature body of sons in Christ's Image. "Behold, what manner of love the Father hath bestowed upon us, that we should be called the sons of God: therefore the world knoweth us not, because it knew him not. Beloved, now are we the sons of God, and it doth not yet appear what we shall be: but we know that, when he shall appear, we shall be like him; for we shall see him as he is." (I John 3:1-2). The sons of Jair also refer to a people out of this world according to the Word. This is the believer's hope!

The thirty sons rode on thirty ass colts. Ass colts mean they *have been broken to a load*. The root means to *lift up* a master. No matter the angle, ascension in power is the order of the day. As sons we are able to bear up under any load because we move in His Strength. The ass colts represent a mature vehicle by which the King comes into His City, the New Jerusalem! The sons of God will bear our Master only. We will not take up any other burden. When Jesus was ready to make His triumphal entry into Jerusalem, he had to get the colt from the village near them. The vehicle could not come out of tradition but from another place which is not identified.

Lastly, the thirty sons had thirty cities. Thirty cities speak to a city of perfection. Leaving the principles of the doctrine of Christ, let us go on unto perfection

(Hebrews 6:1). John saw the holy city, New Jerusalem, coming down from God out of heaven, prepared as a bride adorned for her husband (Revelation 21:2). A city is so called by its being frequented by people. It is a guarded place of excitement. Many are waiting for events to take place in natural Jerusalem that have already taken place in the Spirit. New Jerusalem is now above and free.

Jair's possession is a heavenly possession. The Bible says the cities of the sons of Jair are called Havoth-jair which means *a life-giving place* unto this day. This is why the new convert needs a local church that is a place where the Life in Christ is constantly ministered. All that Jesus accomplished for us and as us through His Cross is then experienced in us by the power of His Spirit. The experiential learning associated with Jair's judgeship, lands one in flow of the out-working of Christ by His Spirit. Now it is easier to understand why the Holy Spirit inspired Jairus to be called by name, for in his name, the Nature of the Spirit is captured.

Fast forward to the miracle of raising the son of the widow of Nain. We find only that she is a widow without mentioning her name. The intricacies of the Wisdom of God continue to be seen in His Holy Word. The word widow simply means *deficiency.* The root meaning of deficiency is *gulf, chasm, or great opening.* The only other place the root meaning is found in the New Testament is in the Parable of the Rich Man and Lazarus.

These three miracles parallel three-fold things in Scripture. Among those three-fold things are the major feasts of the Old Testament: Passover, Pentecost and Tabernacles, which is an excellent study. Presently, it is a great time to note the striking relationship between the root meaning of widow and the great interval, *(chasm, gulf or great opening)* separating the Feast of Pentecost and the Feast of Tabernacles. The raising of the widow's son symbolizes Pentecost and the Feast of Tabernacles or Ingathering is symbolized by the raising of Lazarus. Backing up for coherence, the raising of Jairus' daughter symbolizes Passover. Passover was celebrated on the fourteenth day of the first month on the Hebrew Sacred Calendar, Pentecost was celebrated 50 days after Passover, and Tabernacles was celebrated beginning the 15th of the seventh month. This information may cause one to appreciate the gap or chasm aforementioned.

When reviewing the Parable of the Rich Man and Lazarus, the chasm or great gulf will be seen with higher definition spiritually. Although not the Lazarus from our third miracle, the Holy Spirit is leading His elect on to something glorious with the usage of this name. As a reminder, Lazarus means *God has helped.* The related Scripture is Luke 16:19-31. In the raising of the widow's son, the Holy Spirit reveals to us that a great gulf was spanned.

Upon reflection, the young man had to be awakened to the truth of the power of the Gospel. Like Paul, he has to be persuaded that neither height nor depth shall be able to separate him from the love of God which is in Christ Jesus our Lord (Romans 8:38-39). Like Peter, he must learn that he cannot call common what God has called clean (Acts 10:15). He must learn the Law of Moses and the Prophets spoke of Jesus (Luke 24:44). He must understand that if he will not believe the writings of Moses that he cannot believe the Words of Jesus Christ our Lord. The young man must indeed understand that only in Christ are we Abraham's seed, and there is neither Jew nor Greek, bond nor free, male nor female, but all are one in Him (Galatians 3:28-29).

In the raising of the young man, the widow's son, all *deficiency* is consumed by the all sufficiency of God (Second Corinthians 3:5). This young man further represents the working of the law of the Spirit of life in Christ Jesus in the believer. The highest law now begins to operate in the child of God. The period between Pentecost and Tabernacles gives time for this law to be written on one's heart. In the young man's very being, he comes to know what the law could not do, because it was weak through the flesh. He will experience God sending His Son in the likeness of sinful flesh, and for sin, condemning sin in the flesh that the righteousness of the law might be fulfilled in us who walk not after the flesh, but after the Spirit. There is now no condemnation to be leveled against him (Romans 8:1-4).

Like Paul the Apostle, he learns that God is pleased to reveal His Son in him that he may preach Christ (Galatians 1:16). This power of God in Christ is able to take a Hebrew of the Hebrews, a Pharisee *(rich man)* (Phillipians 3:5) and makes him a minister to the heathen *(beggar)* thus counting all his credentials but dung for Christ. The young man raised by Jesus sees true riches as unsearchable in Christ, and the gulf of restriction transformed into the depth of the riches both of the wisdom and knowledge of God!  Just when the young man thinks he has learned all there is to know during this spiritual stage of development, he is shocked into realization as he discerns how unsearchable God's judgements are and His ways past finding out! (Romans 11:33).  This glorious power makes the *rich man* travail in birth until Christ be formed in the *beggar* (Galatians 4:19).  What a Bridge over the gulf! All blessings and honor to Christ Jesus our Lord!

Key witnesses to Lazarus' resurrection were his sisters, Mary and Martha.  The meanings of both their names center in one word, *rebellion*.  The meaning of their names sums up the cause for man's separation from God in the first place.  How great the gulf was fixed until Jesus came! As previously seen, the rebellious one was fully dealt with in the Cross.  The raising of Lazarus after four days necessitated an intervention only the Resurrection and the Life could execute.  After being raised, Lazarus speaks to the new man who is to ever be with the Lord.

*To him give all the prophets witness, that through his name whosoever believeth in him shall receive remission of sins.*

Acts 10:43

# CHAPTER 20

JESUS IN ACTION
PART 4

(JESUS' LOCATION PRIOR TO A DEATH DENYING MIRACLE)

In this section, we will concentrate on the location of Jesus prior to each death-denying miracle He performed. Referring back to Mark 5 we will restart with the raising of Jairus' daughter whom we have previously layered. Each coating of these miracles shows us the depths of the riches of Christ. Beginning with verse 21 which reads, "And when Jesus had crossed again in the boat to the other side, a great crowd gathered about him; and he was beside the sea." The location of Jesus when Jairus approached Him concerning his daughter is now clear. He was *beside the sea*. As intimated earlier, the Scriptural accounts of each of the resurrections during Jesus' earthly ministry contain Life-giving detail for eyes that see and ears that hear. His location is speaking volumes one would be wise to inquire into.

The *sea* as used here means *salt*. The only other occurrence of its meaning is captured in the Gospel of Mark, Chapter 9. Verse 49 reads, "For every one shall be salted with fire, and every sacrifice shall be salted with salt." Historically, salt was used as an antiseptic and to prevent fermentation. For acuity of the importance of Jesus' location and what it means in connection with the raising of Jairus' daughter, let us examine the first occurrence of salt recorded in the Bible. It is found in the Leviticus 2:13 which states, "And every oblation of thy meat offering shalt thou season with salt; neither shalt thou suffer the salt of the covenant of thy God to be lacking from thy meat offering: with all thine offerings thou shalt offer salt."

Continuing, in Numbers 18:19-20 we learn, "All the heave offerings of the holy things, which the children of Israel offer unto the LORD, have I given thee, and thy sons and thy daughters with thee, by a statute forever: it is a covenant of salt for ever before the LORD unto thee and to thy seed with thee." Salt makes a covenant inviolable. This means the alliance cannot be dissolved. Our greatest need is an understanding of and an appreciation for God's mighty clutch on each of us. We are firmly in His mighty Hands.

Many of us have experienced the ease with which relationships disintegrate in our society. Because of such encounters, it is sometimes hard to imagine God's eternal Love. Our Heavenly Father wants our experience to change. Rather than having to imagine the surety of His covenant that was ratified with the Blood of Jesus, He wants us to experience His great Love through a relationship with Him. God changes not. Earthly relationships may end, but God's promise and His oath are immutable and His Love is everlasting.

Following is an excerpt from 2 Chronicles 13 that outlines the lasting power of a *covenant of salt*. In this passage Abijah addresses Jeroboam who declared war against him. Abijah's dependence was upon God and His Word. His address began with a question, "Don't you know that the LORD, the God of Israel, has given the kingship of Israel to David and his descendants forever by a covenant of salt (2 Chronicles 2:13 NIV)?" He ended with the declaration of God Himself as Captain of Judah because they did not forsake Him. Of course we know the result, "and God delivered them into their hand" (2 Chronicles 13:16) despite the fact that Jeroboam had twice the number of men of war.

Jesus' location when approached by Jairus assures us of His great love for us. It proves the New Covenant is one of salt and that salt is Jesus Himself. That is why He declared, "Have salt in yourselves and have peace with one another." (Mark 9:50). As living sacrifices unto God we are *salted with salt*. Jesus gave us an example of assurance when he lifted up Jairus' daughter by the hand paralleling His being lifted up on the Cross, drawing all men unto Himself.

In the next miracle when Jesus raised the widow's son, again, His location sheds light on Who He is and what that means to us as believers. Look intently at the place where Jesus is confronted with the death of the young man. Remain mindful that this young man represents a stage of spiritual development where we arise or wake out of sleep. One is awakened to Whom God is and progress to maturity begins. Not only does one begin to learn of God at this stage, there is also an understanding of whom we are in Him. Again, Luke 7:11-12 reads, "And it came to pass the day after, that he went into a city called Nain; and many of his disciples went with him, and much people. Now when he came nigh to the gate of the city, behold, there was a dead man carried out, the only son of his mother, and she was a widow: and much people of the city was with her."

Jesus was nigh to the gate of the city of Nain. Nain means *pleasant*. The root meaning of Nain is *pasture* or *the abode of a shepherd*. This information is going to prove valuable for us in this miracle and that of the raising of Lazarus. Jesus is at the *gate* or door of a *pasture*. In John's Gospel, Jesus announced that He is in fact the *Door of the sheep*! Additionally, He is the Good Shepherd! We are the abode of the Good Shepherd. John Chapter 10 clearly distinguishes the shepherd from the hireling. The shepherd enters by the door.

Finally, we come to the miracle of raising Lazarus, the full grown man. Let us go to the Scripture containing the account right away. We learn from John 10 then John 1 where Jesus is abiding. The Jews sought to take Jesus after accusing Him of blasphemy. John 10:40 states he went away again beyond Jordan into the place where John at first baptized and there he abode. In John 1, the place where John baptized is named Bethabara which means *house of the ford*. (John 1:28). A *ford* is a place where you can walk across water. We see then Jesus is located beyond Jordan at Bethabara. Jordan means *the descender.*

This location speaks to the full grown son and must be spiritually discerned. Jesus is the fulfillment of our crossing Jordan as He descended from glory to rescue us from the penalty of sin. He is the *Ford* or Crossing whereby we go over Jordan *dryshod* as Israel did under Joshua (Joshua 3:17). Dryshod means *closed up.* As in Song of Solomon we are to our Beloved "*a garden enclosed; a spring shut up, a fountain sealed.*" (Song 4:12). He has taken us back to the Garden which would be incomplete without a *fountain*. Hallelujah!

John the Baptist said of our Lord, He that cometh from above is above all: he that is of the earth is earthly, and speaks of the earth: he that cometh from heaven is above all. Again, He cometh from above. To revitalize our memory of previous points, that is the same as saying He *descended* which is the meaning of *Jordan*. "*Above*" means *from the beginning, a higher place or from on high*. The verse goes on to clarify that above is actually *heaven*. Jesus Christ, the Descender is the Baptizer with the Holy Ghost and fire. The Descender *testifies*! That means He *bears witness; experiences something seen and heard; taught by revelation and has a report*! The prophet Isaiah understandably asks, "Who hath believed our report? And to whom is the arm of the LORD revealed" (Isaiah 53:1).

God in Christ has accomplished a work of righteousness that makes all things new. The higher law of the spirit of life in Christ Jesus sets one free from the law of sin and death. Second Kings 2 gives us a glimpse of what Christ has done through His obedience unto death, even the death of the Cross. It is amazing that as we look at the ministry of Elisha, one can see Christ and ourselves in Him! As it is written, if one could receive it, Elijah's return was fulfilled in John the Baptist. As pointed out, Jesus came back across Jordan to raise Lazarus, demonstrating Himself as Head and Body. See it now and see it always! We are the Body of Christ, and it is He Who does greater works through us, His submitted Body.

Reviewing, Elisha's words prove He saw what he needed to see at the departure of Elijah. He said, "My father, my father..." As noted, that is the same as saying, "Abba Father" (Mark 14:36 and Romans 8:15), which denotes the words of a son. A FULL GROWN SON as depicted by Lazarus. A full grown son goes on to perfection unto the measure of the stature of the fullness of Christ. Like John the Baptist, this son has decreased and Christ has increased. Corruption has been swallowed up of incorruption! Glory to God, our Heavenly Father. As we review these events repeatedly, begin to picture yourself as a believer returning from beyond Jordan empowered by the Spirit of Christ, one in whom Father and Christ make Their abode.

*Elisha's second miracle of healing the water* connects to the miracle of Jesus raising the widow's son. As we concentrate on Jesus's location in connection with these resurrections, we penetrate deeply into spiritual understanding of His great, all-encompassing love for us. As a reminder, Nain means *pleasant.* If you recall, the men of Jericho called the situation of their city *pleasant.* Jericho's history describes it as a place where the walls kept the people shut up. None could go out or come in. Spiritually, it speaks to the bondage of the carnal mind. During the spiritual stage of growth of the young man, Jesus deals with the carnal mind and presses down the walls of it with His Mighty Hand. That is why Jesus said, "Young man, arise" or wake up to your new mind, the Mind of Christ.

In this present picture with Lazarus, the full grown man, we see a son of God in the Power of the Spirit dealing with a spiritual situation as Elisha. A *pleasant* place but "the water is naught and the ground barren." Is that not a replica of a carnal mind? The carnal mind is unable to produce anything because the water (word) is naught making the ground (person) barren. The carnal mind is at enmity with God and His Word; therefore, a son of God must live through the Power of Christ.

Because God has done a new thing in Christ, the man of God must use a *new cruse.* Of all things, remember Elisha put *salt* in the cruse and cast the salt into the waters and they were healed. (Did you connect the importance of *salt* and how it speaks of Christ here to our earlier survey of Jesus' location by the sea (salt) preceding the raising of Jairus' daughter?) The key here is that every stage of spiritual growth is rolled up into the ministry of the full grown son. Just as Elisha reversed the course he came with Elijah, so we see the reversal with the *pleasant* city (Nain and the young man) then to the *salt* (the sea and the child). In response to Elisha's ministry God then declared, "there shall not be from thence any more death or barren land."

As we capture yet one more powerful thought, refer to Elisha going to Bethel (*house of God*) from Jericho. Remember too, on the way little children, which according to Hebrew language means young men, mocked him. Pointing to those at an immature stage in their spiritual walk, they mocked Elisha to provoke him to attempt to do what God had done to Elijah by taking him up in a whirlwind. The mockery expected to see the Power of God at the whim of man. As established, when it says Elisha *cursed them*, it is not in the sense readily assumed.

*Cursed* means *to be light or bring into contempt.* These young men brought judgment upon themselves because Elisha, now a son of God, merely reflected God's Light in their presence, bringing instant judgment to all that is unlike Him. When this happens, flesh has to be dealt with, hence, two she bears came and tore them. Jesus Christ, the Son of God, will be the only one left standing! Full grown sons minister Him from a position of rest like Lazarus who was found seated at the table with Jesus (John 12:2) after Jesus raised him from the dead.

One final point of recall is that from Bethel, Elisha went to Carmel meaning a *fruitful garden.* Hopefully, the Spirit brought to your remembrance that we are a *garden enclosed* in Christ. This further represents our complete restoration in Christ Jesus our Lord. Elisha then proceeded on home to Samaria which means *watch station.* Isaiah 21:1-9 tells us what the watchman sees. "Babylon (confusion) is fallen, is fallen." Revelation 18:2 states John, who was in the Spirit, heard the same glorious truth from the angel or messenger that came down from heaven. This angel is described as having great power and the earth was lighted with his glory. Surely in Christ, in that all-powerful place of Spirit, Babylon the great is fallen, is fallen! Not going to be, but rather *is fallen*! Consider your location, dear reader. Walk in the Spirit!

*Touch not mine anointed, and do my prophets no harm.*

*Psalm 105:15*

# CHAPTER 21

## THE WAY OF THE SPIRIT

To help shore up the minds of serious believers until the Mind of Christ is securely in place, an Old Covenant picture will be laid out under the glorious Pattern of Jesus Christ by His Spirit. Immediately following the lifting up of the brazen serpent in the wilderness, God allowed the journey of the children of Israel to take a course that would reveal the Holy Spirit's power in the spiritual journey of every believer. If one chooses to walk after the flesh, this information will not help at all. As repeatedly warned, this truth must be seen through the eyes of the Spirit. No matter where a believer is on his or her spiritual journey, these truths concerning our Lord Jesus Christ and the power of the Holy Ghost are going to lighten the way in a spectacular fashion. May the reader be strengthened with might in the inner man and the eyes of your understanding enlightened by the Spirit of Christ!

Numbers 21:1  And when king Arad the Canaanite, which dwelt in the south, heard tell that Israel came by the way of the spies; then he fought against Israel, and took some of them prisoners.

21:2  And Israel vowed a vow unto the LORD, and said, If thou wilt indeed deliver this people into my hand, then I will utterly destroy their cities.

21:3  And the LORD hearkened to the voice of Israel, and delivered up the Canaanites; and they utterly destroyed them and their cities: and he called the name of the place Hormah.

21: 4  And they journeyed from mount Hor by the way of the Red sea, to compass the land of Edom: and the soul of the people was much discouraged because of the way.

Following a powerful "mountaintop" experience of victory wherein their enemy was utterly destroyed, the "soul" of the people became discouraged because of the way. The "way" is the Lord Jesus Christ who said, "I am the way, the truth and the life." As we see a picture of our spiritual journey in these verses, it is important to note that it was the *soul* of the people that was discouraged. The soul is the part of us that contains our mind, will and emotions. The flesh is motivated by this part of our being, and it is wise to note how the Holy Spirit inspired the soul to be the focus at this point. Discouragement will always be magnified in the soul. This is why we must walk in the spirit so as not to fulfill the lusts of the flesh.

We will liken this stage to when we all heard the Gospel and learned of the victory of the Cross but made no real commitment to Christ. It was the stage when the soul was jockeying for the superior position within us and our concentration was on the things that made us feel good in the sensual and temporal realm. Many experienced life-saving victories and still refused to yield to God and serve Him. It is wise to note that the attention span of the soul is very, very short when it comes to spiritual things. See how quickly the people forgot the recent victory. Although they were journeying by the way of the Red Sea (which should have been a constant reminder of God's delivering power), they could not meditate on God's goodness because of the overwhelming power of the sinful soul.

Numbers 21:5 And the people spoke against God, and against Moses, Wherefore have ye brought us up out of Egypt to die in the wilderness? For there is no bread, neither is there any water; and our soul loathes this light bread.

Jesus taught the multitude concerning this very bread that natural Israel loathed in the wilderness. According to John 6:31-35, "Our fathers did eat manna in the desert; as it is written, He gave them bread from heaven to eat. Then Jesus said unto them, Verily, verily, I say unto you, Moses gave you not that bread from heaven; but my Father giveth you the true bread from heaven. For the bread of God is he which cometh down from heaven, and giveth life unto the world. Then said they unto him, Lord, evermore give us this bread. And Jesus said unto them, I am the bread of life: he that cometh to me shall never hunger; and he that believeth on me shall never thirst."

God's provision is always spiritual. It does not matter that we look at its natural effect alone. Everything God does has an eternal effect because He is eternal Spirit. By providing a constant diet of manna during their natural wilderness walk, God was showing in type that Jesus Christ is enough to sustain us in our spiritual walk. They actually "loathed" God's provision. Before we gasp in awe, think of what place our blessed Lord has in our own lives even now. To loathe something means they were sick of it and disgusted with it. They even called it "light bread" which means there was nothing satisfying about it. That is precisely what the unsaved soul thinks of Jesus Christ. The unregenerate man finds Him disgusting and unsatisfying. Jesus only? Yes!

Numbers 21:6 And the LORD sent fiery serpents among the people, and they bit the people; and much people of Israel died.

21:7 Therefore the people came to Moses, and said, We have sinned, for we have spoken against the LORD, and against thee; pray unto the LORD, that he take away the serpents from us. And Moses prayed for the people.

21:8 And the LORD said unto Moses, Make thee a fiery serpent, and set it upon a pole: and it shall come to pass, that every one that is bitten, when he looketh upon it, shall live.

21:9 And Moses made a serpent of brass, and put it upon a pole, and it came to pass, that if a serpent had bitten any man, when he beheld the serpent of brass, he lived.

When the soul is in control of man, it sins by murmuring against God and rebelling against His ways. The wages of sin is death. Consequently, God sent fiery serpents that bit the people and caused them to die. Notice upon their true repentance, God put a provision for life in their midst. Is that not what happened to us as believers when we repented of our sins and meant it in our hearts? They did not have to do anything of themselves but believe God's Word and do what He commanded. Let us read John 3:14-17 and see what God was orchestrating through His people way back in the wilderness for our learning.

"And as Moses lifted up the serpent in the wilderness, even so must the Son of man be lifted up: That whosoever believeth in him should not perish, but have eternal life. For God so loved the world that He gave His only begotten Son that whosoever believeth in Him should not perish, but have everlasting life. For God sent not His Son into the world to condemn the world; but that the world through Him might be saved."

Consider it a requirement to understand the context of John 3:14-17. It is in the middle of Jesus' response to Nicodemus concerning the New Birth and is part of a direct answer to Nicodemus' question of "How can these things be?" The new birth is a completely spiritual transaction. That is why Jesus said to Nicodemus, "That which is born of the flesh is flesh; and that which is born of the Spirit is spirit." The natural man will never be able to understand such things without the help of the Comforter. Remember Nicodemus' response of reentering his mother's womb, and he was a *teacher* in Israel. Many teachers and preachers today still fail to understand the spiritual transaction of the New Birth because it is spiritually discerned, and they are not Spirit-filled.

Jesus Christ was the fulfillment of the Brazen Serpent in the wilderness. Notice God told Moses to make a "fiery serpent" just like the ones that were biting the people. Jesus completely identified with our sin nature in the Cross. Drawing the force of sin into Himself, our sins were carried away. We were crucified together with Christ according to Galatians 2:20. We died with Him, and we were buried with Him as it is written in Colossians 3:3, Romans 6:4, and Romans 6:8.

Because Jesus took on our sin nature to be sacrificed for us and as us, He had to go to hell. Praise God we do not have to go to hell because we have already been there and done that in the Lord Jesus. He was quickened or made alive in spirit and according to Colossians 2:13, and we were quickened with Him. When He was raised so were we because the Bible declares it in Colossians 3:1. Now we are seated with him in heavenly places as announced by Paul in Ephesians 2:6. We must look upon Him and live! People will not have that opportunity if His Gospel is not preached to them!

Let us go back to Chapter 21 of Numbers. Note that immediately following the lifting up of the brazen serpent, the people took a course of journeys that speak powerfully of our walk of faith by the power of the Holy Spirit. Deep is calling unto deep therefore, pray for God to reveal His Word unto you. Nothing about it is complicated, it simply must be spiritually discerned.

Numbers 21:10, And the children of Israel set forward, and pitched in Oboth. At the first stop after repentance and looking on the Brazen Serpent, the children of Israel came to a place call Oboth which means water skins. A water skin is a vessel for holding water, somewhat like a wine skin. For the believer, after saying yes to Jesus, we are now ready to hold water. Just what does that mean? Perhaps we can get powerful insight from the words of our Lord in John 7:37-39. "In the last day, that great day of the feast, Jesus stood and cried, saying, If any man thirst, let him come unto me, and drink. He that believeth on me, as the scripture hath said, out of his belly shall flow rivers of living water. (But this spake he of the Spirit, which they that believe on him should receive: for the Holy Ghost was not yet given; because that Jesus was not yet glorified)."

Do you see the amazing parallel? Upon experiencing the New Birth, the very next stop is the infilling of the Holy Spirit. We must be filled with the Spirit, otherwise we will not be able to grow spiritually. We will not be able to understand spiritual things. We will not be able to testify of Jesus. We should be mirroring His works. Jesus said He would send the Comforter or the Holy Ghost, and He would lead and guide us into all truth. Friends, truth is a Person and His Name is Jesus!

Numbers 21:11, And they journeyed from Oboth, and pitched at Ijeabarim, in the wilderness which is before Moab, toward the sunrising. From the point of our being filled with the Spirit, the next place is *Ijeabarim*. It means the *ruins of Abarim*. If you are familiar with your Bible, you may remember that Abarim was the mount the Lord called Moses to in order to view the land of promised possession of the children of Israel. This place, Ijeabarim, or ruins of Abarim tell us a great deal if we have ears to hear. Ruins at the place of viewing the Promised Land speaks to the demarcation point where the believer must come to the end of all self-help during the spiritual walk. Our personal views, isms, and schisms on spiritual matters must be brought to ruin as we fully embrace's God's view and adhere fully to it.

Everything now depends totally upon God. According to the Scriptures we are sons if we are led of the Spirit of God. We cannot be led of the Spirit and do what we want to do at the same time. God is so wonderful to put this place of spiritual growth after the infilling of His Spirit. Remember, we cannot do it alone but through Christ we can do anything. Did you catch the spiritual fact that coming to the end of self is at the same time spiritual growth? In fact, it is a quantum leap for the believer. The old man or old nature was crucified with Christ but he still tries to run things because he trained the flesh. Well, as new creatures in Christ, we have a new trainer called the inner man and he takes all his instructions from the Holy Ghost.

Numbers 21:12, From thence they removed, and pitched in the valley of Zared. Next we come to a place called *Zared*. It means exuberant in growth. Notice spiritual growth spiraled upward after the coming to the end of self! Bear in mind that it takes much water or Holy Spirit to grow at this rate in the ways of the Lord. Paul said to the church at Ephesus that Christ loves His Church so much He gave Himself for us that He might sanctify and cleanse it with the washing of water by the word. Exuberant growth in the Body of Christ means we are becoming glorious to Him as He desires.

Numbers 21:13, From thence they removed, and pitched on the other side of Arnon, which is in the wilderness that cometh out of the coasts of the Amorites: for Arnon is the border of Moab, between Moab and the Amorites. The next stop is *Arnon*, and it means a brawling stream. We have determined by the Holy Spirit that water speaks to Himself. It is amazing at the number of places that mean water or some form of it during these moves. Notice how the Holy Spirit inspired every detail to be captured with each location. Here is a place where the believer must be cautious because despite the power of the Spirit, there is temptation lurking close by. Arnon borders Moab. Moab speaks of ease. Woe to them that are at ease in Zion! It was also a place of famine. Remember Ruth who was a Moabitess? She left her people to follow her mother-in-law, Naomi, back to Bethlehem-Judah, or the house of bread and praise. That is where she met her kinsman redeemer, Boaz, who is another profound type of our Lord Jesus Christ.

Arnon is between ease and the Amorites who were mountain dwellers. Mountain dwellers should cause the believer's spiritual antennae to go up at once. During our spiritual walk, the battle is always in the mind. Think about it. The enemy's number one game plan is to talk us out of who we are in Christ. It is the same old game as in the Garden. Do not forget the mind is in the realm of the soul! In II Corinthians Chapter 11, Paul cautions that church of his fear that as the serpent beguiled Eve through his subtilty, so their *minds* could be corrupted from the simplicity in Christ. Stay focused and centered on Christ when you come to the place Arnon speaks of.

Numbers 21:14, Wherefore it is said in the book of the wars of the LORD, What he did in the Red sea, and in the brooks of Arnon,

21:15, And at the stream of the brooks that goeth down to the dwelling of Ar, and lieth upon the border of Moab.

Here is the reinforcing reminder of the Holy Ghost of His power. Notice how His power takes us to the dwelling of Ar. *Ar* means city. The Psalmist reminds us that there is a river the streams whereof make glad the city of God. It is called the holy place of the tabernacles of God. A tabernacle is a dwelling place or house for God. The Scriptures declare that Jesus is a Son over His own house, whose house are we! God is also in the midst of the city the Psalmist saw in the spirit. We shall not be moved because God will help us and that right early. His Word declares it! Alleluia! Of course we will not move on without reminding ourselves again that Ar borders Moab. Moab not only speaks of flesh but also of *ease* (Jeremiah 48:11). The elect of God would be fooled only if it were possible.

Numbers 21:16, And from thence they went to Beer: that is the well whereof the LORD spake unto Moses, Gather the people together, and I will give them water. Beer means a well. Yet another place of drawing out water or even more of the Holy Spirit! Notice here the LORD commanded Moses to gather the people. This brings to mind the Feast of Tabernacles or the Feast of Ingathering. What a harvest of souls is being realized in the earth today! Many are waiting on a move of God yet He is moving moment by moment in the power of His Spirit. Let us stop gazing up and go up! We are no longer living but Christ lives through us!

Numbers 21:17, Then Israel sang this song, Spring up, O well; sing ye unto it: One of the features of the Feast of Tabernacles is that it is a feast of joy! In I

Peter Chapter 1, the following verses reveal the reason for such joy. "Blessed be the God and Father of our Lord Jesus Christ, which according to his abundant mercy hath begotten us again unto a lively hope by the resurrection of Jesus Christ from the dead, to an inheritance incorruptible, and undefiled, and that fadeth not away, reserved in heaven for you, who are kept by the power of God through faith unto salvation ready to be revealed in the last time. Wherein ye greatly rejoice, though now for a season, if need be, ye are in heaviness through manifold temptations; that the trial of your faith, being much more precious than of gold that perisheth, though it be tried with fire, might be found unto praise and honour and glory at the appearing of Jesus Christ: Whom having not seen, ye love; in whom, though now ye see him not, yet believing, ye rejoice with joy unspeakable and full of glory: receiving the end of your faith, even the salvation of your souls."

Glory to God for salvation of the soul! The soul that once loathed Jesus becomes fully submitted unto Him through the power of the Holy Ghost. Soul is feminine in Scripture. David said, "My soul shall make her boast in the Lord." The soul or the woman becomes submitted to her husband, the inner man or the spirit man. "She," the soul that is, becomes the Proverb 31 woman. She no longer has to be told to keep silent in the church. She knows her husband, and he rules his house well. She is now a help meet for her husband, the inner man, who was completely saved the moment the believer said yes to Jesus!

Numbers 21:18, The princes digged the well, the nobles of the people digged it, by the direction of the lawgiver, with their staves. And from the wilderness they went to Mattanah: *Mattanah* means gift or reward. It may sound familiar since it means the same as Matthias who replaced Judas Iscariot among the Twelve. Jesus said in The Revelation, "And behold I come quickly; and my reward is with me, to give every man according as his work shall be." When Jesus walked the earth in public ministry, the disciples asked Him what they must do to work the works of God. Jesus said in John 6:29, "This is the work of God, that ye believe on him whom he hath sent." Lord help our unbelief! What a relief! His yoke is truly easy and His burden is light.

Numbers 21:19, And from Mattanah to Nahaliel: and from Nahaliel to Bamoth: From our reward we go to *Nahaliel* which means valley of God. The root meaning is a mighty stream! Once the Holy Ghost is received, He carries us throughout the journey. God is Spirit and they that worship Him must worship Him in spirit and in truth. As He spoke by the prophet Zechariah, not by might nor by power but by His Spirit! Jesus' earthly ministry was so powerful because He moved in the fullness of the Spirit! We are in this world but not of it. Ours is a life in the Spirit fueled by the Resurrection Life and Power of Jesus Christ. *Bamoth* means heights. It is a present truth that we are seated in heavenly places in Christ Jesus, and that He has blessed us with all spiritual blessings of heavenly places. Sons of God are awakening to our inheritance in the Person and Finished Work of the Lord Jesus Christ.

Numbers 21:20, And from Bamoth in the valley, that is in the country of Moab, to the top of Pisgah, which looketh toward Jeshimon. *Pisgah* means a cleft, which is a place of protection that looked toward Jeshimon meaning the wilderness. When we look back and see where it is that God has brought us, we see the supernatural power with which we came over. Only the perfect Sacrifice could have delivered us from such an experience. Only God can get the glory as we look back and see the enemy confounded and utterly destroyed on our behalf. Experience after experience was to teach us His ways. He knows the make-up of the soul and what it takes to save it. His ways are not our ways. His thoughts are not our thoughts.

Continue the story if you like and see that what follows is great victory over the mountain dwellers or Amorites. The weapons of our warfare are not carnal but mighty through God to the pulling down of strongholds. Again, the warfare is in the mind. That is why every thought must be brought captive unto the Lord Jesus Christ. If our thoughts do not line up with our victory, we have not put on the mind of Christ. He knows precisely what is true of us in Himself, and that is the way Father sees us. Yes, from Father's view we are complete in His Son. Do you believe it? Remember your reward is based on your works, and your only work is to believe on the Lord Jesus Christ.

*Above all, you must understand that no* **prophecy of Scripture** *came about by the prophet's own interpretation of things.*

*2 Peter 1: 20, NIV*

# CHAPTER 22

## ENTER INTO HIS REST

Nearly twenty years ago, I had the wonderful privilege of being in a glorious gathering for a series of meetings. Among us were holy men and women who have been walking with God and ministering unto His people for many years. One of the weathered warriors who had ministered for over 45 years imparted a prophetic word to me which I knew beyond a shadow of doubt was from the Lord. He simply said, "God has raised you up to live in His sight. Follow on to know Him." Only the inner man can fathom life from God's perspective while fully seeking Him to a point of total intimacy. The spiritual exchange reverberated throughout my being, and I left those meetings changed and with a renewed sense of destiny. When the spirit is touched by The Spirit, the individual cannot help but respond with awe and urgency.

Later, I got a surprise phone call from this wonderful servant and messenger of God, and we reflected on the awesome power of God in those meetings. He went on to share how he had just come out of more meetings where he had never seen the power of God in such a manner in all his years in the ministry. Savoring every word of our holy conversation, one statement emerged most revelatory and powerful. Surprisingly, he stated that he no longer felt the need to preach like he had been doing in the past. His statement held such profound truth not so much in what he said, but what I heard loudly said in my spirit. We have entered into the *rest* of God.

The Body of Christ everywhere is sensing this powerful truth. People of God are beginning to realize that if we are to ever see His glory manifested in us, we must come to a complete end of ourselves so that Christ alone ministers. May I impose upon you to envision what it shall be like when all of us are fully yielded and the only thing proceeding from us is Christ! Words like "my" and "mine" will be replaced with "His."

My husband, Paul so aptly stated once, "What if we stop saying what would Jesus do and start acting on what Jesus did!" Herein may lie the problem for many because of a lack of understanding of what Jesus did. In order to ever *rest*, we must get an understanding of what Jesus did and act on it. Jesus, the Christ of God, knew no sin but became sin for us. Through complete obedience to the will of the Father, He went to the Cross and became a curse so that He could do away with the force of sin that separated us from God.

By becoming the very curse that held us captive, we were drawn into Him. Back to the serpent on the pole, He fully identified with sinful nature. Through His death, the Lamb of God reversed the curse with His atoning Blood. His death was our death. Death could not hold Him because He is the Resurrection and the Life. He was raised from the dead with all power. He completely destroyed the works of the devil. When He was raised from the dead, we were raised with Him, as He was the Head of a new creation. There was no longer only the old Adamic nature. Christ, the last Adam and the life-giving Spirit brought forth a new nature.

We act on what Jesus did by making Him Lord of our lives and following Him. His death was our death and His life is our life. The problem arises when we live our lives apart from Him. Again, His life is our life or stated differently, He lives His life through us. It is not Him and us living in the temple that we are. It is He alone who lives in us. His life is a total existence in complete obedience out of the plan and will of God. There was never an instance where Jesus did what He wanted to do, but He did only what He saw Father do. The work is finished! Enter into His *rest* for it is a *rest* driven by resurrection power! No force can stand against such power and authority! May I impose one last time? *Believe in Him* that we may have life and that more abundantly.

*Son of man,* **prophesy** *against the prophets of Is-rael who are now* **prophesying.** *Say to those who* **prophesy** *out of their own imagination: 'Hear the word of the LORD!'*

*Ezekiel 13:2, NIV*

# CONCLUSION

Jesus is our Life and Future. This whole thing is about growing up into the measure of the stature of His fullness (Ephesians 4:13). The Holy Spirit has been given so there is no reason why false prophets should have as much presence as they do. We have the Power in Christ to eradicate the nonsense of false prophecy in the Church. The Apostle Paul wrote vital instructions in 1 Corinthians 2:11-13 saying, "Who knows a person's thoughts except their own spirit within them? In the same way no one knows the thoughts of God except the Spirit of God." If we are to know what God's thoughts are, we must hear them by His Spirit! The psyche of a man or woman will not work in such matters. Paul went on to say that what we have received is not the spirit of the world, but the Spirit of God, so that we may understand what God has freely given us. When one does not understand what we have been freely given, he will attempt to "buy" it, and the hireling knows that very, very well. We must speak in words taught by the Spirit of Truth and not with man's wisdom.

By the Spirit the essence of the prophetic from God's perspective will be seen. The Spirit of Truth is the Ability that accurately describes or predicts what happens to us in Christ. He can accurately recount what took place in and by the Spirit in the Work of the Cross. He can show us how Christ has been made unto us wisdom, righteousness, sanctification, and redemption ( I Corinthians 1:30). It is by His Power that we eat butter and honey or the spirit of the Word which is revelation knowledge so we will know to refuse the evil and choose the good (Isaiah 7:15). His shed Blood made us kings and priests unto God and Father in Whom we minister after the Order of an Endless Life. No, the false prophet cannot reveal these magnificent truths to a believer because there is a place in God the buzzard or dead flesh eater does not know.

One can expect prescient or predictive ability by the Spirit. It is not possible for the elect to be fooled so what can overtake us? The vantage point of Divine Spirit is far-seeing. Instruction, warning, and blessings unlimited! As we are faithfully perched in Christ, the Spirit uncovers as He wills and takes of His and shows Him unto us at our Heavenly Father's good pleasure. Sons and daughters prophesying or preaching infallibly not by might nor power but by the Spirit of God.

Apocalypse is a wonderful word for the believer. There is not a scary thing in it. It merely means uncovering or unveiling as in the Revelation of Jesus Christ. We know the true blessing of reading and hearing that great Prophecy! In Christ, the distortion of documentaries with man's finite wisdom and Hollywood movies have not invaded our hearts with fear or uncertainty. Not even books written by so called "prophets" move us in the least because we know our position in the Resurrected Christ. We speak the wisdom of God in a mystery, even the hidden wisdom, which God ordained before the world unto our glory. (1 Corinthians 2:7). In Spirit, the mystery is fully exhibited and crystal clear to anointed eyes and ears.

How could such a powerful blessing be forfeited for such a pathetic imitation? Simple answer, because people have underestimated the Power of the Holy Spirit. They do not know our God. When He says by My Spirit, that is what He means! Man has substituted a powerful ministry of the prophetic with a watered-down message that arouses pity making it seem as though God's people are vulnerable to a devil who is out of control. Sadness has replaced the joy of the Lord for many solely because of the message of the false prophet. Human emotions powered by flesh out of control have put a wretched, heartbreaking, pitiful church on display under the guise of the Church of the Lord Jesus Christ.

Instead of the Power of the Gospel of Jesus Christ, a miserably inadequate message of self-help has invaded the Church and become the norm. Can one not see its inadequacy and insufficiency? Listen to many of the songs and testimonies of defeat? How is the Almighty God glorified in such pathetic worship and praise? Too many ministries are so feeble none can be helped through them. A controlling spirit with sarcastic inflections of voice is not power. It is weak, sensual, and devilish. The false prophet's actions are deplorable and contemptible and God is not pleased. Moving the passions of people is not the object of true ministry. That is a clear sign that a carnal ministry is in high gear. Instead of sorrow and grief there should be righteousness, peace and joy in the Holy Ghost. Repent!

To ministers of righteousness flowing in true prophetic ministry with Christ securely at the helm, may God bless you all with spiritual blessings in heavenly places found only in Christ. As the Apostle Paul prayed for the Ephesians, may God give you a spirit of wisdom and revelation in the knowledge of Christ; the eyes of your understanding being enlightened; that you may know what is the hope of his calling, and what the riches of the glory of His inheritance in the saints, and what *is* the exceeding greatness of his power toward us who believe, according to the working of his mighty power which He wrought in Christ, when He raised Him from the dead. May your ministries be blessed as you guide God's people into the fullness of Christ, and the Spirit of Truth be your constant Companion while enjoying the liberty in found only in Him. So be it!

# ABOUT THE AUTHOR

Carolyn P. Bynum is the founder and pastor of Restoration Christian Ministries Center, Sierra Vista, Arizona. Pastor Bynum is an anointed teacher sent to the Body of Christ. She has been ministering for more than two decades. Her media ministry reaches most of the USA and several other nations. Her dynamic teachings may be heard anytime at www.youtube.com/VeryChrist. Her local radio outreach has blessed the local community and outlying areas for more than 20 years. She is a Spirit-filled, ordained minister and noted conference speaker. Pastor Bynum is also a musician, lyricist, and arranger who has written numerous praise and worship songs. She served 21 years of honorable active military service in the Army and retired as a Chief Warrant Officer Three with numerous decorations, commendations and citations from both wartime and peacetime. She has a Bachelor's Degree in Behavioral Science from Western International University and a Master's Degree in Counseling from Chapman University. Pastor Bynum wants the world to know that, like the Apostle Paul, the Gospel she preaches is not of man neither was she taught it, but it pleased God to reveal His Son, Jesus Christ in her. Pastor Bynum and her husband, Bishop Paul E. Bynum, Sr., travel together and minister the Gospel of Jesus Christ in the Power of the Holy Spirit. They have two sons and four grandchildren.

## SIX STEPS TO THE THRONE

### *King of Kings*

### 6. SEATED IN CHRIST

And hath raised us up together, and made us <u>sit together in heavenly places in Christ Jesus:</u>
Ephesians 2:6

### 5. RAISED WITH CHRIST

If ye then be <u>risen with Christ</u>, seek those things which are above, where Christ sitteth on the right hand of God.
Colossians 3:1

### 4. QUICKENED TOGETHER WITH CHRIST

Even when we were dead in sins, hath <u>quickened us together with Christ</u>, (by grace ye are saved;)
Ephesians 2: 5

And you, being dead in your sins and the uncircumcision of your flesh, hath he quickened together with him, having forgiven you all trespasses;
Colossians 2:13

### 3. BURIED WITH CHRIST

Therefore we are <u>buried with him</u> by baptism into death: that like as Christ was raised up from the dead by the glory of the Father, even so we also should walk in newness of life.
Romans 6:4

## 2. DIED WITH CHRIST

Now if we be <u>dead with Christ</u>, we believe that we shall also live with him:
Romans 6:8

For ye are dead, and your life is hid with Christ in God.
Colossians 3:3

## 1. CRUCIFIED WITH CHRIST

Knowing this, that our old man is <u>crucified with [him]</u>, that the body of sin might be destroyed, that henceforth we should not serve sin.
Romans 6: 6

<u>I am crucified with Christ</u>: nevertheless I live; yet not I, but Christ liveth in me: and the life which I now live in the flesh I live by the faith of the Son of God, who loved me, and gave himself for me.
Galatians 2:20

But God forbid that I should glory, save in the cross of our Lord Jesus Christ, by whom the world is crucified unto me, and I unto the world.
Galatians 6:14

# About the Publisher

Let *Life to Legacy* bring your story to literary life! We offer the following publishing services: manuscript development, editing, transcription services, ghost-writing, cover design, copyright services, ISBN assignment, worldwide distribution, and eBook conversion.

We make the publishing process easy. Throughout production, we keep the author informed every step of the way. Even if you do not have a manuscript, that's not a problem for us. We can ghost-write your book from audio recordings or legible handwritten documents. Whether print-on-demand or trade publishing, we have packages to meet your publishing needs. At *Life to Legacy*, we take the stress out of becoming a published author.

Unlike other *so-called* publishers, we do more than just print books. Our books and eBooks are distributed to book buyers, distributors, and online retailers throughout the world – this is real publishing! Call us today for a free quote.

**Please visit our website**
www.Life2Legacy.com

**or call us**
877-267-7477

**Send e-mail inquiries**
Life2Legacybooks@att.net